Job Interview

Achieve the Job You Has Always Waited for With 35 Powerful Interview Questions and Answers

(Overcome Anxiety and Improve Your Social Skills With the Best Strategies and Expert Tips)

Richard Pollak

Published by Rob Miles

Richard Pollak

All Rights Reserved

Job Interview: Achieve the Job You Has Always Waited for With 35 Powerful Interview Questions and Answers (Overcome Anxiety and Improve Your Social Skills With the Best Strategies and Expert Tips)

ISBN 978-1-989990-64-3

All rights reserved. No part of this guide may be reproduced in any form without permission in writing from the publisher except in the case of brief quotations embodied in critical articles or reviews.

Legal & Disclaimer

The information contained in this book is not designed to replace or take the place of any form of medicine or professional medical advice. The information in this book has been provided for educational and entertainment purposes only.

The information contained in this book has been compiled from sources deemed reliable, and it is accurate to the best of the Author's knowledge; however, the Author cannot guarantee its accuracy and validity and cannot be held liable for any errors or omissions. Changes are periodically made to this book. You must consult your doctor or get professional medical advice before using any of the suggested remedies, techniques, or information in this book.

Upon using the information contained in this book, you agree to hold harmless the Author from and against any damages, costs, and expenses, including any legal fees potentially resulting from the application of any of the information provided by this guide. This disclaimer applies to any damages or injury caused by the use and application, whether directly or indirectly, of any advice or information presented, whether for breach of contract, tort, negligence, personal injury, criminal intent, or under any other cause of action.

You agree to accept all risks of using the information presented inside this book. You need to consult a professional medical practitioner in order to ensure you are both able and healthy enough to participate in this program.

Table of Contents

INTRODUCTION 1

CHAPTER 1: AFTER APPLYING FOR THE JOB 4

CHAPTER 2: REVIEW THE JOB POSTING 9

CHAPTER 3: SELL YOURSELF LIKE A PRO 17

CHAPTER 4: CREATING YOUR PERSONAL VALUES CHART 36

CHAPTER 5: HOW IMPORTANT IS IT TO HAVE A GOOD RESUME? 41

CHAPTER 6: PURPOSE OF AN INTERVIEW 45

CHAPTER 7: RESEARCH THE COMPANY AND THE POSITION YOU ARE APPLYING FOR 54

CHAPTER 8: DRESS TO IMPRESS 57

CHAPTER 9: THE EXACT PROCESS OF THE INTERVIEW AND HOW IT WORKS 60

CHAPTER 10: PREPARATION 66

CHAPTER 11: QUESTIONS TO BE AVOIDED 76

CHAPTER 12: HOW LONG WERE YOU IN YOUR LAST JOB FOR? 93

CHAPTER 13: TOP JOB INTERVIEW QUESTIONS 99

CHAPTER 14: SELL YOURSELF: DEVELOPING THE RIGHT COMMUNICATION SKILLS 115

CHAPTER 15: COMMON INTERVIEW QUESTIONS AND THEIR BEST 121

CHAPTER 16: PRE-INTERVIEW PREPARATION: PROFESSIONAL STANDARDS 131

CHAPTER 17: WORKING WITH STAFFING COMPANIES .. 149

CHAPTER 18: WARNING SIGNS TO LOOK OUT FOR DURING YOUR INTERVIEW 158

CHAPTER 19: THE JOB INTERVIEW PROCESS 176

CONCLUSION 193

Introduction

Job interviews can be a nerve-racking experience, especially without experience or the knowledge of what to expect. Even the most practiced interviewees struggle from time to time with the interview's format and the unusual questions they encounter. But whatever your age, experience, qualifications, strengths, weaknesses, or current profession might be, mastering your next interview and standing out is an entirely feasible feat, as you've hopefully come to learn.

There are definitely some tried and true approaches to acing an interview. However, the most important things are: Presenting a confident, professional appearance, answering questions with honesty and integrity, and Being Yourself.

In this book you will learn how you can answer common interview questions from the basic to the most mind-boggling. You should now have a good understanding of how job interviews are conducted and how to prepare for it. After reading this book, you should be able to ace your next interview and land your dream job with great ease.

I have broken down the questions into different categories. Always ensure you aren't strictly memorizing these answers - they should be authentic and catered to you.

The most important thing to remember at the end of the day is that you should always be yourself. The people interviewing you want to know who you are and why they should pick you above everyone else! Don't stress yourself to the point that you overthink everything in the interview, but be prepared by reading through these questions, answers, and explanations.

Interviews are a strange experience. We're usually asked a series of questions, are expected to respond in a particular yet honest way, and then our responses are analyzed and measured by an individual who decides whether we fit certain criteria. While we do this, we need to present ourselves, our experience, and our skills in a flattering and unique light, but at the same time, we need to make sure we don't sound overly confident in the process. In other words, interviews require a very different way of communicating than we're generally used to. So naturally, mastering the interview takes time and experience.

The candidate that is recognized in the first phase interviewing process is typically the candidate that is apt to find himself or herself on the receiving end of an attractive job offer when the entire interview process is concluded. To come out the victor in the rigorous challenge of interviewing is, without a doubt, only the first of many accomplishments that will be achieved as you move forward on your journey to employment and career success.

Chapter 1: After Applying For The Job

You just applied for a job and now you are waiting to hear about scheduling an interview. What can You do in the meantime to prepare yourself for when you finally get the call to schedule that important meeting? Sometimes there is no time to prepare once you get that call so preparing yourself ahead of time will give you a leg up in the game.

Research the company, position, and industry you are applying to. The interviewer might be curious to know how much work you have put into your job search. Was this something you applied for on a whim or were you actively looking for a job? How do you perceive the companies position in their specific industry? Who are the companies largest competitors? Why does this company have an advantage in its industry?

Go over and make a list of your personal selling points. You need to know yourself as a brand. Having three to five selling points in your head ready to present to the interviewer is helpful for times when you may need a quick response to questions like, "Why should we chose you over another candidate?" Selling points such as why you are the best candidate for the position should have specific you can constantly refer to. Do not forget that the interviewer will want to know why you want this job so mention what you like about it, what rewards it offers that you find valuable, and what abilities are required that you posses?

The interviewers are trying to find reasons to remove people from the screening process. Put yourself in their shoes. What reasons would they have for not wanting to hire you? You do not need to point out all your flaws to yourself and make yourself self conscious but be honest about what types of things the company may find as a disadvantage to having you as an employee. Keep your reasons related to your experience and what the company is looking for in a candidate. Prepare a defense for these points where you may have to admit that you do not have certain experience or requirements but you are willing to learn them and continue working towards achieving what the company seeks. Turn the negatives into a positives.

In the pages of this book we will help you prepare for common interview questions. A quick search on the internet will bring up some of the same questions almost every interviewer uses in some form. You can also search for less common questions and begin preparations for these as well. If you prepare answers to the basic questions you will be less likely to fumble during the interview.

It is one thing to prepare with mental answer but you should prepare out loud as well to make sure what are you trying to say comes across clearly. Practice your answers at least ten times out loud and watch yourself in a mirror or record yourself. This way you can see your body language and hear the tone in your voice.

You may be surprised at what types of things come across from your body that you did not even know you were doing.

The first few times you will sound unprepared and forget what you are trying to say. This is completely normal and exactly why you are practicing. Ask you friends for feedback on your body language as well. If you have a difficult time speaking clearly place a pencil in your mouth and hold it with your lips and teeth, long ways. The pencil should be laying from one corner of the mouth to the other. Begin speaking your answers through and over the pencil. This is called diction. If you are able to understand your responses despite the pencil you are on the right track to speaking clearly. If you mumble this is a good practice for you.

Try doing this reciting nursery rhymes as well. If you have a presentation to give, practice presenting with this technique. While you will not be doing this for real in your interview, practicing your diction will ensure you have clear and understandable speech. This tactic is used in theater but is a great way to remove issues with mumbling or slurring words. It can also help remove any thick dialects and begin the process of having a standard American accent which is also helpful in phone interviews where the interviewer does not have context clues.

While you want to practice speaking, do not try to sound to rehearsed or polished. The practice of speech and presenting will help you not only in interviews but also in your job. Most positions require some form of human interaction. You do not want to sound as though you are regurgitating a prepared speech or lines out of a book. Do your best to answer naturally but the practice of speaking will allow you to work on ensuring your clarity without ruining the spontaneity of your responses.

Chapter 2: Review The Job Posting

What's in a job posting you ask? Everything you would need to know about who the company is looking for. A good part of finding job interview success depends on applying to the right jobs. If you have been applying to pretty much any job available under where the sun shines for you, you are not very likely to find a lot of success. You will only be wasting a lot of valuable energy and would be resorting to template applications, cover letters, and interviews. However, if you would only invest a small fraction of that time thoroughly reading and understanding a job description, you can go on to apply to the jobs most suited to your skills and thus have higher chances of success. Following are a number of things you should be focusing on when going through a job posting:

The Job Title: Almost every job posting has this, but not a lot of job-seekers take a good look at it. An editor's assistant and assistant editor might sound pretty similar, but there is a world of difference in their duties, qualifications, and skills. Be sure to dissect the job title word by word and truly understand what the said company is specifically looking for. You should be adding this job title in the subject line when sending in your resume and cover letter. There is a fair chance that the company is hiring for multiple jobs, and adding these specifications makes it easier for the recruiters to assess your application better. Not adding the job title could make it look like you are simply mass mailing your application and haven't really understood the requirements of the job.

Qualifications/Requirements/ Experience: This section explains in detail about what the company is really looking for. You would see details like the minimum education required, minimum prior experience, and other soft and hard skills needed for the job. It is not

necessary to be able to tick all the boxes here, but you should feel that you are familiar with the skillset and understand the kind of employee the company is actually seeking. Focus more on the qualifications than the interpersonal skills. You may be a great 'team player,' 'motivator' and have great 'dedication,' but if you don't know how to code data or sketch a house plan, then there is a good reason you aren't a good fit for the job. Before they tell you the same after you focus so much of your time and energy on it, better you figure it out on your own.
Responsibilities: This bit describes what you are supposed to do at the job. Dissect it properly. Is it something that you believe you can handle or would enjoy doing? Do the responsibilities match with what you have done on your previous jobs? Don't be discouraged if you haven't been responsible for exactly the same tasks at your previous workplace. There may be little variations, and the company would be more than accommodating if you are otherwise a great fit. However, if the

responsibilities don't make sense to you, then better stop reading further.
About Us: This is pretty self-explanatory. Most jobs provide a background on the company. Take this as the first step to learn more about the company. Research further via the company's website, social media presence, and other portals to understand the company's environment and culture.
Pay and Benefits: Salaries are often not stated in the job post unless the job is based on hourly salaries. You may see statements like 'starting from xxx' or 'competitive salary' or 'salary commensurate with experience.' Benefits, on the other hand, are openly stated since they are pretty much the same for all employees.

Experience: This bit outlines the level of experience required to apply for a job. Some may be looking for fresh graduates to train themselves while other jobs might require at least a number of years of experience. The salary and responsibilities vary for the same job depending on the level of experience. But if the job posting asks for three to five years of experience and you only have two years of experience, by all means, apply anyway. This requirement only means the company is not looking to train someone. And with two years of experience under your belt, you may just be the candidate they are looking for. Some job postings would specify what sort of experience they are specifically looking for. It may say something like 'three years of bookkeeping experience' or 'ten years of industry experience,' you better not ignore these. If they have bothered to be this specific, then they have a very good idea about the candidate they want to hire.

Reading Between the Lines

You can decode a lot about a job posting by focusing on small things. For instance, if the post states "other duties as assigned," then it means that the manager isn't very sure about the duties that will be assigned. This means you can talk about how you are flexible and accommodating and would love the opportunity to be assistive in the company's growth. Similarly, if the job post uses words like 'must-have' or 'required' then this means they aren't very flexible about the candidate they are searching for, so if you don't much that criterion, better not apply. On the other hand, words like 'preferred' and 'desired' skills may not be deal-breakers, but having them would just give you an edge over the other candidates.

It may not always be possible to meet all the requirements on a job posting; it is not that necessary either. They are just a window into what the company is actually looking for without telling much about themselves. You will be a good judge of whether or not you can be a good fit for the company. If you are unable to decide, searching for the company online may help you make a wiser decision. Knowing more about the company will help you decide whether or not you see yourself adjusting to the environment. It is only when you can convince yourself that you would be able to convince the company that you are indeed the most suitable candidate for the job.

How Badly Do You Want it?

You have checked the job description, thoroughly dissected it, and understand what the company is looking for. Now is the time to ask yourself if you really are the right candidate. Do you have the skills for it? Do you meet all the criteria? Do you see yourself happily working there? Will you be able to adapt to the company's culture and enjoy it? How do you see yourself contributing to the company's growth in the long run? These are just some of the questions that you need to answer even before you can even begin the application process. These questions will help answer the million-dollar question of 'how badly do you really want it' and also will help you construct a more targeted and motivated cover letter. So even if you lack a few requirements, your determination and desirability will help you stand out among the other candidates.

Needless to say, avoid sending in applications at places that don't excite or motivate you. Don't apply to three dozen places within two days just to get out of unemployment. The lack of motivation and effort in penning down the cover letter will become evident and will greatly diminish the chances of you landing a good job. The term quality over quantity applies to the number of jobs that you apply to too. Better apply at one job with all your heart and determination than sending off template cover letters to a dozen places.

Chapter 3: Sell Yourself Like A Pro

The job market today is more competitive than ever. Think of it this way:

It's easy to advertise a product when there are fewer competitors. All you need to do is to show the product to the consumer (example: show potential consumers an image of a bath soap and they'll buy it because they know what it's for.) However, if there are several similar products on the market, showing the consumers an image of the product is not enough to convince consumers to buy it. You have to remind them what it's for, how it will make their lives easier/better, and all the other reasons why they should buy it (this is when you start using commercial models, the perfect script, perfect background music, perfect packaging, etc.) More importantly, you have to show potential consumers why your product is better than all the others. It's for this reason why TV and printed ads strive to be more colorful, more interesting, and more unique.

And with the number of job-seekers out there, this is exactly how you should sell yourself as well.

What makes a great salesman great? It's when he's able to take control of the situation while making the clients believe that they're the ones in control. An experienced salesman will discuss the needs and concerns of the clients while persuading the customers that what he's selling is the answer to their problems.

A job interview is no different. View the interview as an opportunity to make a sale. You take control and then subtly guide the interviewer into making you a job offer. Your main goal during the interview is to transform yourself in the eyes of the interviewer from a total stranger to someone that his company must buy.

Listen actively

One of the greatest misconceptions about interviews is that it is the interviewee's moment in the spotlight where he can speak as much as he wants to about himself. On the contrary, active listening is twice as important as speaking in interviews. While a chatty candidate's enthusiasm to please the employer may seem amusing, it doesn't always result to a productive interview. Simply put, it's not about how much you say but how much value your words contain.

Listen closely to what the interviewer says about his business/organization. Your responses must be based according to his company's needs. This way, you turn from being a job applicant to a partner who's eager to share ideas and solutions.

Be on the lookout for conversation builders

From time to time, the interviewer will say some things that you can use to build an interesting conversation.

Example:

Interviewer: "The low inventory turnover is one of our biggest problems."

Applicant: "I understand completely. I've had experience in finding solutions for low inventory turnover in my previous position. Exactly what type of problems are you facing at the moment?"

Mirror

When you listen, don't just sit there like a cold marble statue. This would embarrass or offend your interviewer. Worse, it might send the message that you're not that interested in the job after all. Respond through your body language. Nod in agreement from time to time. That said, don't exaggerate your responses by agreeing to every single thing that the interviewer says. You must have your own opinions. Even so, restrain yourself and put your opinions on hold long enough to hear the interviewer out. You may not 100% agree with what the interviewer is saying, but play your cards right by finding a common ground and taking it from there.

Example:

Interviewer: "I think _____ is highly important. To accomplish this, we must use Approach A or Approach C."

Applicant: "I certainly agree that _____ is of primary importance. And I also favor approach C. While I can see the advantages of using Approach A, have you considered trying Approach B?"

Interviewer: "Why?"

Applicant: "Well, based from my experience, one of the greatest advantages of Approach B is..."

Lean forward slightly or sit at the edge of your seat to communicate to the interviewer that you find the exchange stimulating. Practice the art of mirroring the interviewer's message. This means that you match his/her tone. When he's excited about something, reflect his enthusiasm. When he adopts a serious tone while discussing a certain topic, reflect his seriousness.

Important: Limit your use of mirroring techniques, especially when it comes to mimicking your interviewer's body language.

It's true that mimicry may serve as a social glue that can assist in the promotion of rapport between human beings. In fact, years of research has proved that generally, subtly mirroring another person's tone, vocabulary, words, posture, and gestures can make you seem more likable to that individual. However, more than one recent study by psychological researchers reveal that when it comes to job interviews, mimicry must be kept to a minimum, especially when there is more than one interviewer.

In an experiment done by scientists from University of California, San Diego, several mock interviews were recorded. In the interviews, some of the participants mimicked the interviewers' gestures while others did not. After this, the scientists asked judges to watch the videos and measure the interviewees' level of competence, likeability, and credibility. The result? The judges found the candidates who kept mirroring to a minimum to be more competent, credible, and likeable.

A similar study was conducted by a team of experts at Texas Tech and Drew Universities. According to the study, mirroring can have negative effects on an applicant's success. This is because humans mimic not only positive gestures but also negative gestures as well. In other words, if your interviewer happens to find you less likeable or if he's just having a bad day, mirroring his gestures, his facial expression, or his tone of voice will only cause you to send a negative message to his subconscious. You become a living mirror of his negative emotions. Seeing you reflect how he's feeling inside will only serve to reinforce his negative perception of you.

Therefore, use mirroring strategies sparingly. Instead, concentrate on using body language to convey confidence and enthusiasm. You already have a lot on your mind during an interview and this is one less thing that you should worry about.

Repeat and rephrase

Rephrasing is one way to prove to the interviewer that you've been listening to him attentively. Like mirroring, rephrasing must be kept to a minimum. Make sure you restate only the most important points to the interviewer.

Example:

"If I understand you correctly…"

"From what I understand, you're saying that…"

Remind the interviewer why you're there in the first place

This may seem a bit frustrating, but in case the interviewer comes unprepared, his rambling thoughts may lead the conversation into an unpredictable path that will hinder you from selling yourself most effectively. At this point, your job is to give him a little nudge back to the right direction.

Example: "I just can't tell you how excited I am to be here. I believe that what I have to offer could be of use to this company."

With a statement like this, you're placing the focus back on the reasons why you're the right person for the job.

You might come across an interviewer who likes to monopolize the conversation. Should you butt in? Definitely. How else would you be able to have the opportunity to sell yourself?

But how do you interrupt a talkative interviewer's monologue without seeming rude?

First, absorb what you can from the interviewer's words. What you're actually listening in for are conversation builders and opportunities to highlight your selling points. Once it comes out of your interviewer's non-stop mouth, pounce on it.

Example:

INTERVIEWER: "As I was saying, one of the biggest challenges in this business is to guarantee sufficient cash flow--"

APPLICANT: "Allow me to interrupt you for a second. What you're saying is just too interesting. Management of cash flow is actually one of my main areas of interest. I have a couple of fresh ideas which you might be interested in hearing and I can't wait to hear your thoughts on them…"

Another type of interviewer you might come across is the stressed out, overworked type. He/she may be distracted during the whole interview. He/she may even cut you short to answer phone calls. Instead of feeling indignant, express your sympathy. Then, use it as a way to bring up the value that you can add to the company.

Example:

"Wow, you really are very busy during this time of the year. I know what it's like and I can totally see why the company could use someone with my skills and experience."

This will direct the interviewer's attention back to you.

Remember: There are times when the job interviewing task falls on a chiefly technical person. When this happens, you get an interviewer who will lead the conversation into a discussion of technical matters. While it's important to demonstrate your technical know-how, it is also necessary to remember that this isn't all that your interviewer wants to know about you. Naturally, he'll also want to know what you would be like as an employee. Chances are, he may be having a hard time communicating what he really wants to ask you. The solution? Look for a way to connect your technical skills with your transferrable skills. Provide examples of situations where you used both.

Keep in mind the lessons that your high school teacher taught you

Whoever said that high school subjects have no practical application in real life wasn't familiar with the rules of successful interviews. Remember when your grammar school teacher kept hounding you about using a substantial topic sentence, an engaging introduction, and a powerful conclusion in your essays? Well, you have to follow the same rules when answering interview questions.

Open with your topic sentence. Then, proceed with statements that support the topic sentence. Finally, end with a conclusion that summarizes your point.

Example:

"I understand that it's my job to find out and cater to our potential clients' needs, which will, in turn, enable me to INCREASE the company's sales. This is why I made it my business to help the company to earn ____ dollars in sales last quarter. I was able to persuade former clienteles such as

_____ and ____ to purchase the company's most recent products. I also secured new clients such as _____ and _____. Moreover, I collaborated with _____ and _____ departments to help draw more attention to the company's flagship product, which is _____, and thus, maximizing its visibility to potential consumers. Within one year of being in the company, I increased the company's sales by ____ % through diligence, social skills, salesmanship abilities, and by being a team player."

Phrases that Keep the Ball Rolling

Using the following magic phrases will aid in maintaining the momentum of the conversation:

"I agree…"

"I can certainly relate…"

"That's interesting…"

"We should talk about…"

"Tell me more…"

"We should pursue that further…"

"That's also one of my biggest concerns…"

There are also phrases that could stop a conversation dead in its tracks. Here are a few examples of what you must avoid:

"Definitely not…"

"I absolutely disagree…"

"There is no way…"

"It's impossible…"

"It's final…"

"That's not how it should be done…"

Be on the lookout for 'Buy Signals'

You'll know an interviewer is interested in you when he starts using phrases such as the following:

"Sounds great."

"Interesting."

"I like that!"

Buy signals like these are signs that you've successfully caught your employer with your hook. Now it's time for you to reel him in, proverbially speaking. You do this by expounding on the idea that captured his interest. That said, unless they're really, really impressed, interviewers are rarely expressive. Often, their buy signals come in the form of a request for you to elaborate further on the topic.

Example:

"Can you tell me more about…"

"I'd like to hear more about…"

"Let's go back to…"

"Would you care to be more specific about…"

Now, most interviewees would dread the idea of being asked to speak more about a certain topic. Since you're reading this book, you shouldn't be feeling this way any longer! This is an indicator that you've hit the right button. But what is the correct way of expounding on an idea?

In marketing, a product's features refer to the characteristics of the product (ex: portable, compact, etc.) If you're a product, then your features are your skills (ex: great managerial skills, reliable, trustworthy, etc.) On the other hand, a product's benefits refer to the positive things that it can do for the user (ex: portable, compact materials can be used while on the go and are easy to store.)

It's your features that will catch the interviewer's attention. To draw him in, you now have to present your benefits. In other words: How can your skills make the employer's business/life more profitable/better?

Example:

"I believe that the most important part of my position as an assistant manager is to provide you with more time to pursue higher responsibilities. My goal is to support you in the management of the store so you can have more valuable time in your hands."

Make a closing statement that closes the sale

You're playing the part of a salesman. This means you're not leaving the interview room without urging the employer to seal the deal.

Wrong: "So, did I get the job?"/"Did I do okay?"

This comes across as overly presumptuous, pathetic, and perhaps worst of all, needy. You're likely to end up with the standard dismissive response: "Don't call us. We'll call you."

Correct:

"Based on all that I've told you, don't you think I would be a great fit for the company?"

This part can be quite tricky. You need to make use of a closing statement that will actually extract a positive answer from the employer. To use or not to use closing statements like this will depend on how well you've established rapport with your interviewer and how effectively you were able to answer the interview questions. If you have a good feeling about the interview, proceed to prompt the employer into action. If not, follow a different route:

"Thank you so much for your time, Mr./Mrs./Ms. _____. It has been great pleasure and I do believe I have a great deal to offer to this institution. But please, if there's anything that I wasn't able to discuss to your satisfaction, do let me know. What could I tell you to encourage you to make a proposal?"

Keep in mind that it's not about pressuring the employer to make a decision on the spot. This is about increasing your chances of urging the employer to commit to you positively. Closing statements like these suggest a hint of urgency without the sense of impatience or desperation. It simply reminds the interviewer of your value.

Chapter 4: Creating Your Personal Values Chart

To help you to narrow down what your most important personal values and needs are within your career is a chart for you to fill out which will help you to narrow down your choices. You will choose from a scale of 1-5 with 5 being the most important. Below are three sections within this chart that will help you to find out what your most important values are to have in your dream job.

Intrinsic Values – Satisfaction/Motivation at Work

1) How important is Variety and Change at work

2) Being an Expert

3) Working on the Frontiers of new discoveries

4) Aiding or helping others such as training

5) Be involved in helping society

6) Excitement/Adventure

7) Physical Challenges/taking risks

8) Need to feel respected for your work

9) Be competitive with others

10) Be in direct contact with public

11) Have influence on others

12) Do work that involves precision

13) Need to gain a sense of Achievement

14) Want to be able to express your Creativity

15) Want to work doing good positive and beneficial things

Extrinsic Values – these are such things as rewards or bonuses that are given at work, earnings, pay increases, job titles. People often stay at a job they do not like but they want the paycheck that it offers. This is known as the golden handcuffs.

1) Authority, control, power

2) Being able to Travel with job

3) Get monetary rewards or bonuses

4) Need to be an entrepreneur

5) want to work as a team player

6) Work in an environment that is upbeat and fast paced

7) Having steady regular work hours

8) Set your own hours or flex time

9) Be wealthy

10) Have social status

11) Need to have Intellectual status

12) Getting recognition through rewards such as bonuses

13) Work Union

14) Work in a pleasing environment such as outdoors

15) Work in a high-risk environment

Lifestyle Values

Being able to choose how and where you will live and what you will do or how you will spend your leisure time. How important are these lifestyle values to you.

1) Save money

2) Going on expensive vacations

3) Having access to education

4) Being an active member of your community

5) Living in an area with access to sports facilities

6) Be able to entertain at home

7) Being Active in Politics

8) Live a simple lifestyle

9) Need to be able to spend quality time with family

10) Have to be located in big city

11) Like to live abroad

12) Personal growth is important

13) Being a homeowner

14) Live in a rural area

15) Enjoy your life at work and at home

Choose five of the most important values from each list then take these 15 and choose the top 5 of them. Then take these top five and write a few sentences to summarize what your important values are to you in your home and work life. This exercise can really help you to find a career that suits your personal values it is also a great tool to use in preparing yourself for an interview.

Chapter 5: How Important Is It To Have A Good Resume?

The resume plays a big part in the job application. Do you know a job offer that does not ask you to submit your resume?

It is impossible to apply for a job without submitting a resume.

It is always on top of the requirements you need to submit so employers will have a first glance on what you have to offer for the position you are applying for. It can be dropped to different offices personally when you are in dire need of a job. Resumes are also sent through the use of internet via email or social media networks. It is very important that your resume is clean and presentable. It should be made really well for the employers to have interest on your job application.

It is now called "Resume"!

Gone are the days of the "bio-data" as what it was called in the earlier years. You don't have to buy it from bookstores or just from a small retail store. That printed form called bio-data is printed with fixed questions that makes your answers simple and without relevance. A good resume must be done the proper way.

You have to be guided by these tips for you to catch the employers' attention and interest!

Keep it short – you are living in the modern world where people are too busy. Employers don't have much time reading your long resume. It is not for them to go through your resume when they see that it is done in 4 pages. The moment they see it, they lose their interest and it is disappointing to know that your resume might go to the trash bin. A simple yet full of sense resume is the one that employers like. Make your resume short but smartly done. Make sure that every important detail is included but you don't have to explain everything. If they see a good resume you will have the chance to be called for an interview. So it is now your chance to talk about the information you have on your resume.

Send it as PDF – there are other types of formats to which you can send your resume. The technology introduces a new format every now and then but the best of them all is the PDF format. It may be considered as the oldest type but it is applicable to most of the computers. Do not make employers take more of their time to open your resume because it is possible that they will proceed to the next one. There are many job applicants and they won't bother fixing their computers just to open your resume and they won't make their computers lose its format settings either. It can be harmful to their system.

Close strong – you don't have to use many words in closing your resume. Finish it in a second or two so you can avoid repeating useless words.

Just keep in mind that your resume should be made short, but meaty. Send it in PDF format, finish it quickly and you are sure to get a job very soon!

Chapter 6: Purpose Of An Interview

The main purpose of a job interview is to provide an opportunity for an employer and a job candidate to meet to determine if a mutual fit exists between the candidate's skills and experience and the organization's needs.

As a job candidate, you should use a job interview to:

Showcase your skills and qualifications in connection with the position

Demonstrate your enthusiasm for the job and a strong fit with the company

Determine whether or not this position suits your career goals and objectives

Evaluate how well the corporate culture matches your values and interests

When You are Invited to Interview:

Clarify who you will be meeting with

Ask about length of interview

Obtain a full job description, if available

Inquire whether any company handout information is available

Write down the date and time of the interview

Obtain location of interview and directions, if necessary

Ask if any technical testing will take place

How to Prepare for an Interview:

Conduct further research on the company and develop a clear understanding of how you fit with the organization

Know and understand the job description

Identify your key skills, strengths and characteristics that relate to the job

Review your resume to be familiar with all of your experiences that relate to the job

Practice answering interview questions as they relate to the job description

Prepare your own questions to ask the interviewer

What to Bring to an Interview:

Portfolio to carry all of your papers

Copy of your resume

Official transcript

List of references

Copies of any relevant projects or reports

List of 3 or 4 questions to ask at the end of the interview

Pen and extra paper in case you need to make notes during the interview

When Interviewing for a Job, Remember to:

Stay focused on why you should be chosen for the job

Know why you are a good candidate (i.e. know your strengths and values)

Be able to identify your skills and be prepared to offer examples of where you developed them

How to Make a Positive Impression During an Interview:

Pay attention to your personal grooming (hair combed; nails trimmed; clean appearance ; ironed clothes)

Wear professional attire (business suit, dress shirt, matching shoes)

Maintain eye contact

Be aware of and control your non-verbal behaviour

Bring extra copies of your resume and a copy of your transcript

Plan to arrive 15 minutes early

Offer a firm handshake

Answer questions concisely and directly

Avoid insincere flattery, bravado and cockiness

Present yourself in a positive & professional manner

Let your enthusiasm for the position shine through

Useful Tips for Answering Interview Questions:

Never volunteer any negative information to the employer, unless specifically requested to do so then include what you learned or gained from the experience

Be able to provide concrete examples of your skills from your educational, work or extracurricular experiences

Try to read between the lines - think about what is really being asked

If you don't understand the question, ask for further clarification

If you need a minute to think about your answer, request this of the interviewer to avoid any awkward silences

Know yourself - your strengths and values

If you are interviewing with more than one person, be sure to include all interviewers when answering questions by making eye contact with everyone

Understand the theory behind behaviour based interview questions

Standard Format for an Interview

Although the length may vary, most interviews follow four standard stages:

1. Greetings & Introductions

Introduce yourself and shake hands with each interviewer

Interviewer's goal is to utilize small talk to make you feel comfortable, calm and more relaxed in an effort to prepare you for the next part of the interview

Your goal is to make a strong first impression with your manners, body language and smile

Allow the interviewer to guide you on when and where to take a seat

2. Question & Answer Period

Interviewer may begin with a brief description of the job responsibilities and the organization's plans with respect to the position

Prior to beginning with their list of questions, an interviewer may begin with a general request for you to tell them a little bit more about yourself (give a brief one minute overview of your background and be sure to connect this closely with their company and the job you are applying)

Interviewer will ask you questions to determine whether or not you can do the job and how you will fit into the organization

Through this process, interviewers are also testing your communication and interpersonal skills

Your goal is to answer all questions effectively to clearly demonstrate your fit with the position

Listen closely to what the interviewer is asking you to ensure that you eliminate any doubts they may have about your suitability for this job

3. Opportunity for You to Ask the Interviewer a Few Questions

Have 3 or 4 questions prepared to ask the interviewer that demonstrate your understanding of the position and the company

Ask questions about potential projects, training, supervision, performance evaluation and corporate goals

Use your questions to highlight the skills that make you suitable for this position

You can also use your questions to demonstrate the amount of research you have done on their company

Do not ask any questions during the interview that appear self-serving, such as "What will my salary be?" or "Can I have 2 week vacation in July?"

Questions about salary and vacation can be asked at the time a job offer is extended, but they are not appropriate for a job interview

4. Wrap Up

Interviewer may use the last few minutes of the interview to discuss what happens next, such as timelines for hiring or future interview dates

Offer your list of references if the employer doesn't request it

Your goal is to demonstrate your enthusiasm for the position and express interest in their company

Thank the interviewer for meeting with you and shake hands

If you are interested in the position, ask the employer for a business card

Chapter 7: Research The Company And The Position You Are Applying For

Before the interview you should research and find out as much as possible about the company you will be interviewing for. Finding out information about the company automatically you give you a sense of familiarization for the organization. It is proven that people who go over this familiarization process perform much better during the interview as they reduce anxiety and increase their confidence level.

You should find out as much as possible about the below:

- The company's mission.

- Company's history (e.g. Year of establishment).

- Current Company's goals.

- Names of founder and CEO.

- Company's competitors.
- Recent news and events related to company.

Then you should do your research on the specific position and know the description as provided from the company. In more depth you should find out as much as possible for the below points related with the position:

- The average salary for this job within the company.
- The average salary for this job within the industry.
- Specific duties of an employee holding a position as such.

Knowing this information beforehand will also provide you a peace on mind as you will not look anxious on finding this information but instead you will be able to concentrate on the interview process and provide 100% of your focus and mind to the person who will be completing the interview.

Chapter 8: Dress To Impress

Once upon a time, everybody wore a suit and a tie to an interview. However, over the years, our society has become less conservative in terms of what to wear to a formal event. Today, you probably need not wear a suit and a tie to every interview you are attending. In fact, stubbornly doing so may be detrimental to your bid in getting hired.

The reason why this topic deserves a chapter on its own is because what you wear to your interview might be more important than you think. Whether you like it or not, the way you look and dress up is the first thing people will notice about you and first impressions are formed in a matter of seconds!

Interviewers and hiring managers look out for people who dress appropriately because if they put in the effort to look the part, they are more likely to be successful at the workplace and take things seriously. It also shows that you are eager to make a good impression and that you are able to fit into the corporate or company culture snugly. To ensure that you get dressed just the way you should, here are 3 tips to help.

1) Thoroughly research the company's culture – This is the number one rule when it comes to deciding what to wear to an interview. For example, if you are interviewing for an investment banking company on Wall Street, it might see like a no-brainer to get behind a suit. However, if you are interviewing for just a corporate company, then you probably want to do a little more research on the company's culture. If you know anyone at the company you are interviewing with, reach out and ask them. If that is not an option, you can always swing by the company and take a look at how they are dressed for a regular workday, this will give you a nice idea of what to expect. If you really have no clue what to expect, opt for the safer options - white shirt and black pants for men and white top paired with black skirt for ladies.

2) No fragrance or perfumes – Avoid fragrance and perfumes if possible. The last thing you want is for your interviewer to be allergic to scents when you are wearing heavy fragrance.

3) Invest in a pair of comfortable, work shoes – An appropriate, comfortable pair of shoes is often underestimated by many people. Comfortable shoes ensure that you will not be distracted by blisters or discomfort during the interview. Appropriate shoes shows that you pay attention to details.

4) Don't over-accessorize – Wear appropriate makeup and simple accessories. Avoid being over-accessorized because it serves as a distraction to the hiring manager. Be confident and never forget to wear the best makeup – a smile.

Chapter 9: The Exact Process Of The Interview And How It Works

It's not always easy and quick to get recruited. The job interview process can be a lengthy one. Getting hired once and receiving a job offer is typically a thing of the past. Today, many companies are engaged in an interview process, starting with screening interviews, which often take place on the phone, followed by in-person interviews, second interviews, and even third interviews.

In addition to hiring managers, you have meetings with managers, employees and other staff. The manner in which recruitment is done relies on the company and the systems in place of assessing and reviewing potential new hires. Here's an outline of each phase of the interview process, along with advice on the best way to handle each type of interview when you move up the interview ladder to the job offer.

Screening interview

Screening interview is a sort of job interview that is performed to decide whether the candidate has the skills needed to perform the role for which the organization is recruiting. Screening interviews are usually the first interview in the hiring process if the company does not start open interviews where multiple candidates are screened at an open hiring event.

Phone Interview

Employers use phone interviews to locate and hire job candidates. Mobile interviews are often used to limit the pool of applicants who will be accepted to in-person interviews. For remote work, mobile interviews, Skype, or video may be the way you get recruited.

First Interview

The first in-person job interview is typically a one-on one interview between the candidate and the hiring manager. The interviewer will ask questions about the applicant's experience and skills, the history of work, the availability and qualifications of the company seeking the optimal candidate for the job.

Second Interview

A second interview can be a more in-depth one-on - one interview with the person you first met, or it can be a day-long interview that involves discussions with business employees. You can communicate with managers, workers, executives and other employees of the company. Once you're set for a second interview, you're more likely to have a serious job fight.

Third Interview

When you've made it through the first interview, then a second interview you may assume you're through with the interview process, and you'll soon find out if you're going to get a job offer. This is not necessarily the case. You may have to take part in a third interview and possibly more interviews after that. A third interview usually involves a final meeting with the hiring manager and may give you the opportunity to meet more of your prospective colleagues.

Dining Interview

Dining with job applicants allows employers to test your social and interpersonal skills, as well as your table manners, in a more comfortable for them atmosphere. Based on the interview process of the agency you are hiring and the sort of job you are applying for, you may be asked to a lunch or dinner meeting.

Last Interview

The final interview is the last phase in the interview process and the recruitment where you can figure out whether or not you're likely to get a job offer. Here's information on preparing for an interview when you've met the company several times before, and advice on how to handle a final interview.

Preview Interview Questions and Answers

it's important to practice interviewing and be prepared for the usual interview questions you'll be asked during each step of the process. It is also critical that questions are able to be answered by the interviewer.

Follow Up After Each Step in the Interview

Process an email, even though it may seem like a lot of work, especially when you've gone to multiple interviews, it's important to follow up every step of the interview process. In reality, the most important thing you can do is follow up to express your interest in the position and thank the interviewer for taking the time to see you.

Context Monitoring

You can accept a job offer subject to a background check and/or a credit check.

And, a background check may be carried out prior to the organization accepting a position. What the employer finds during the background check may result in you not getting a job offer or removing a job offer.

Job Offer

When you've made it through the often painful interview process, a job offer will be the final step. The job offer may be subject to conditions attached, so please carefully review the terms. Once you approve it, it is necessary to assess the compensation package, decide whether you want to make a counter-offer, and then embrace (or reject) the work offer in writing.

Chapter 10: Preparation

The Preparation stage and Discovery portion of the Presentation stage both have the same objective. Their purpose is to uncover the felt need of the buyer, in this case the interviewers. I'll say it again.

The purpose of Preparation is to uncover the felt need of the interviewer.

There are few things as important as doing your research on a company. Why? Because the felt need that you find during preparation is the one that you are able to practice solving at home.

Sometimes you will get to the meeting and learn in the Discovery process that the interviewers' felt need is different than the one or ones you prepared for. If you uncover a different felt need during the discovery process you must then shift your entire pitch to answering that need, not the ones you prepared for. This adjustment, in the heat of the moment, is challenging. That is why the preparation is so important.

When preparing for a job interview, I like to be prepared for as many potential felt needs as possible. Some common felt needs are:

Fear of being fired

Fear of the company failing

Dream to spend more time with one's kids and family.

Dream of making a lot of money

Dream of a promotion

Fear of having to spend more time at work

These are just a few of the possible felt needs your interviewer might have. What other potential felt needs can you think of?

Know the Company

So how should you prepare? For starters you need to know what the company does. What are their products? Who are their customers? You should be familiar with their history. You don't have to know everything. But you need to have read through their entire website and you need to check out their social media presence. What information has the company made public? This is the information they want people to know. What is their mission statement? What is their vision statement? You should know this before sitting down for an interview.

Is the company a publicly traded company or a private company? Are they international, regional or local?

Have you ever used their products? If so find some positive things about their products that you might talk about if it comes up.

The interviewer will most definitely ask you why you want to work there, and if you can speak about how impressed you are with how they went from last place in a certain market to first or second, it helps. Maybe you will discover they have a very well respected employee training program and you really want to be a part of it. Or you could mention you are intrigued by their work in South Africa or an award they received.

Be sure to take note if the company has been in the news. If it's positive news you might be able to use it during the Discovery stage. If it's negative news be sure you steer clear of that topic.

Know the Job

If you are applying to a job, you need to know exactly what you are applying for. Study the job description listed in the job posting. What are the requirements and responsibilities? It will also give you an idea of the type of answers that they are looking for.

Why does the company need somebody in this job? What happens when this job is performed well? If it's a sales job, then good performance directly leads to increased sales. If it is a customer service job then good performance leads to satisfied customers who are more likely to be repeat customers and who are more likely to refer others to the company.

Does the job produce reports? Who uses those reports? Who needs them to be accurate and why? Who looks good to the higher ups if this job is done well? Conversely, what happens if this job is performed poorly? What happens if the reports are wrong? Whose rear end is ultimately on the line? Who feels emotional stress due to this job going badly? Why do they feel that stress? Who feels euphoria when it goes well? Who gets promoted? Who takes home more money?

I teach people to think like this because these types of questions lead us to the emotions of the interviewers.

You see, it's not just a data entry job that you are applying for. Somebody's fears or dreams are realized based on the performance of this job.

Know Who Will Be Interviewing You

If you can, find out who will be interviewing you. At most companies it will be at least two people. How are these people related to the position you are applying for? Will one of them be your immediate supervisor? Who is the other one? How long have they been with the company? What is their vision for this position and what is their vision for the whole department? Are they rising superstars in the company or are they on two strikes desperately needing to do something special with this hire?

You may not be able to learn these answers until the Discovery phase of the presentation. But try to learn the answers before hand and be prepared. Be sure to check out their LinkedIn profile. If information is limited make some educated assumptions and prepare for multiple possibilities.

Will this be the only interview or are there more rounds of interviews if you do well? Are these interviewers the final decision makers or are they presenting a short list to someone else who will make the ultimate decision?

Do you know the interviewers? Does someone in your network of friends and business contacts know them? If so is it a good relationship or a poor one? Will having that connection help you to build rapport during the interview?

Owners vs. Employees

Owners and employees have different fears and dreams in regards to the position you are applying for. Owners' dreams might include making lots of money, prestige, power, using the business profits to fund charitable causes near and dear to them. They might feel pride in being able to employ dozens, hundreds or thousands who might otherwise be in an economically depressed situation. Their fears might be losing money, letting the community down, or seeing their lifelong work crumble to nothing. Finding this answer will help you present yourself as the solution to their felt need.

Employees might be dream about parlaying a successful hire into their own job promotion. They might dream about a raise. They might be concerned about looking good to their boss. Maybe their hope is that if this job is done well then they won't have to work such long hours themselves and they will get to spend more time with their children. Their fears might be having to work longer hours, spending less time with their children, getting fired or severely reprimanded.

Are you meeting with owners or employees?

So to recap, here are some questions you should be able to answer by the end of your preparation:

- How does the company make money?

- What are their products?

- Who are their customers?

- Can you briefly describe their history?

- What information have they put on their website?

- What is their mission statement?

- What is their vision statement?

- Is the company publicly traded or private?

- Where do they do business?

- What do you like about their products?

- What impresses you about the company?

- Have they been in the news recently? Why?

- Exactly what is the job you are applying for?

- Why is this job important to the operation of the company?

- What happens if this job is performed poorly? Whose rear is on the line?

- What happens if this job is done well? Who benefits?

- Whose labor and decision making depend on this job?

- Who will be interviewing you?

- What are the interviewers' positions in the company?

- How are the interviewers connected to the position you are applying for?

- What do you think the felt needs of the interviewers are? (This is the big one)

- How many rounds of interviews will there be?

- Do you have any personal connection to the interviews?

- Who will make the ultimate decision on hiring for this job?

Chapter 11: Questions To Be Avoided

When I worked for an American company, we were asked to follow a structured pattern of general questions in HR round. Probing into the personal area of candidates is a strict taboo. In India, it appears the interviewer can ask anything that he likes and shoot questions that cross his mind in response to the answers. Generally, one's age, family details, work-life balance have to be noted for analysis. Of course, with limitation that is within decency.

It is not only executives but also managers who usually commit blunders by taking the interview session less seriously. There were times when I recorded the technical round interviews and sent to the US. Any question purported to damage the personal and emotional side could lead to the candidate suing the company.

When I was Head-HR with a construction company in Chennai, I remember the words of its MD who compelled many employees to swap jobs during recession. It appeared highly humorous to watch people bungle while moving across verticals without seriousness. Without mapping their skills, such moves would prove dangerous.

The traditional MD had a general perception that anybody can sit in interview panel, mark attendance, process payroll and disburse salary. I did not allow raw hands to play around the ERP payroll package. Recession time is a boon to set right books, keep records up-to-date and clean.

The interviewee is expected to go prepared and not to ask an interviewer any funny questions. **Get ready for a mischievous humour treat**.

An INTERVIEWEE should not ask the following questions

1) Could you tell me about your organisation?

You are supposed to know about the company before coming to the interview. 'I was too busy in chat and could not browse your site. Sorry! Please tell me sir'. [When you had time to chat, why not browse website? The question is acceptable for genuine reasons.]

2) How many years would it take to go up the next level?

OMG! It appears you are not going to work with sincerity and dedication. So you wanted to scale up in short time? First ascertain whether you are selected or rejected then think about a jump. 'Don't count your chickens.'

3) Do you stress for a medical examination or drug test report?

Why is it you specify 'drug test' and create a suspicion on your own? It might be viewed that you are a person with ill vices.

4) Is salary credited by 30th of the month? Other than salary what else could I claim as reimbursement without bills?

Never show that you are money centric and not job focussed. It could stamp a bad remark as 'squanderer' and 'faker'. Please be aware that corporate companies will never entertain such guys. Wait for the HR person to explain the salary terms and do not initiate. What if it is delayed by a week or month? It is too early to raise such trivial questions.

5) Do you retain inefficient and poor performers or fire them?

If you are a candidate for HR domain position, you may ask so with reference to conversation about performance and appraisal. Never raise a question without a context. It will raise a strong doubt. 'Is the candidate inefficient and useless?'

6) I mentioned two names under References column. Will you call them to cross check for verification?

Why this fear? Hope the names you mentioned are known to you personally but do they know you to recall at appropriate time? It gives a doubt on the authenticity of information you furnished. It is very common for a candidate to call the references and update them. 'Sir, you will get a verification call from ABC. Please do the needful. Also post a good testimonial at my Linkedin page.'

7)Is internet usage allowed liberally or access restricted?

Is this a question worth to be asked in interview? Why do you ask so? You seem to be worried that you cannot spend hours on facebook, twitter, blog, you tube and personal mails. Bad habit!

8)If I don't get selected, what are the other openings suitable?

Always speak about the position for which you applied and are being interviewed. It is not the duty of the interviewer to tell about internal vacancies if any. Is it like asking menu choice in hotels? A Technical

Manager might not be sure about the possibility of openings in his own company.

9)Please tell something about your company's fund position, annual revenue, and share value.

Come on, you are not here to buy the company. Restrict your limit as candidate or go home and Google it. It will make the interviewer uncomfortable and that won't help your candidature.

10) I read in the newspaper that a director of this company was recently caught in a scandal. Is that true?

Are you a candidate or investigative journalist? Imagine if you raised this question unaware to the same person. LOL! Escape.

These are a few typical questions asked by fresh/experienced candidates in the interview. Please strictly follow the dos and don'ts that are told here.

11) Do you encourage 'boomerang' hiring? How many times one can resign and rejoin?

It shows you are keen to join, resign and re join after a gap. Don't expect all companies to follow this concept. Some Call centres do.

An INTERVIEWER should not ask the following questions

In an organisation, an HR Manager has to be the role model to his team and employees as well. Never should his behaviour be tainted and bad mouthed. Just because an opening has to be filled, he should not indulge in giving empty promises to attract the candidate. It is not the time to play his life and career.

If you call this act as recruiting skill, hiring strategy, convincing power or by whatever name, it is unprofessional. The candidate trusts the interviewer and joins the company with high hopes and dream. It is similar to a patient offering to his doctor in whom he has trust. After joining, if he comes to know he had been cheated, it does not take long to abscond and leave the project in the lurch. Who is at loss? It is the recruiter who has to slog and late sit with oily face.

To fulfil his duty an HR manager has sabotaged and done irreparable damage to an employee's career. This is adharma. (Don't guess wild that the author of this book is preaching the Gita. I am always of the view that what you sow is what you reap). You might argue that when it comes to business, telling lies and betraying are common and there is no room for karma theory. You can tell lies as long as it does not deceive him. Tell it frank and if he likes it let him join. Giving false assurances is pretty bad and can damage the image of the company.

As a recruiter if you have roped in candidates for the interview, treat them with respect. Never ill treat and leave them unattended. Be courteous to provide them with coffee and lunch at appropriate time. They have come in solicitation to your call or email. Clear up rounds and make them not to wait unnecessarily. Do not make them get a feel of refugee camp. If you have assured two way fare reimbursement for rail/bus/flight, please settle it on spot. Don't try to cheat him and show empty hands, for he may not come again even if he gets selected. Such was the impression created!

I visualised what sort of answers could emerge out to the so called 'stupid' and 'awkward' questions of the interviewer. Candidates never think twice to fire the impolite interviewer. Let's take a tour.

1) I went through your résumé. You are unsuitable. Why did you come for interview?

Good heavens! I was shopping at the nearby mall when I received a call from your HR department to attend an interview. Having come this far, thought why not I drop in? I also wanted to have a look at the company because I haven't heard of your banner. It's okay. 'My resume please. I don't want to waste it'. [This seems to be a very odd and bitter reaction.]

2) You graduated in engineering. But why did you do courses in CCNA, Import-Export, Photography, Tally and SAP-MM? None of these are related. Don't you have a goal? I say you have no vision.

Sir, how much did you spend on the courses for me? It's time you have to know more about it and not confine to your board room. Learn as much as possible. I say you have no passion.

3) Why should we hire you?

I have been watching your job opening advertisement in the newspaper and job portals repeatedly for the past two months. I wondered why nobody joined so far. At least I thought, let me be merciful to come and attend the interview. Now I understood why none have joined you yet. You are chasing out candidates by asking this foolish question. ROFL!

4)You have so far worked in three organisations. I find a gap of 3 months to 8 months in between. There is no continuity. Is this nice?

Yes sir, not nice. I mean the gaps in your dental arrangement. At least you can fill it with cement but what false data do I have to fill in the gap? Let the career gaps remain. I want to be truthful.

5)We have asked for 0 – 2 years experience in advertisement. You have only 10 months, so we will consider you as fresher.

If you had clearly advertised as 'fresher with 2 years experience only need apply', doubt wouldn't have arised at all.

6)Why you have remained unmarried till now? It is very bad.

Do you have a daughter (or son)? Why not we get into an alliance and clinch the deal? First let me marry and later settle in job. Anyways you are there to get me this job.

7)Miss.Rita, are you going to get married anytime this year? We are planning to groom you as TL to lead a big project.

I would say it depends on my finding an eligible bachelor in this organisation. No worry, finding a groom will also run parallel.

8)Any plans to get pregnant this year? Be clear that we will not relax a single day falling short for maternity leave eligibility.

Not yet decided madam but plans are there to build a design and later abort. I leave it to your choice. Mam, would you mind being a surrogate mother?

9)Where do you see yourself in the next five years from now?

Really I don't know sir. I leave it to god. If I survive the acts of prejudice, demotivation, politics and appraisal, I will let you know where I would be. Now it's too early to answer this.

10) Supposing your boss is younger to you, will you readily accept and cooperate?

This is quite common in foreign companies but might not suit us. With age and experience one becomes a leader else he remains at the lower level. Don't embarrass me to work under small boys.

11) What CTC do you expect? Do you think you deserve it?

Give me INR 6 lakh rupees. Make all fixed and no playing around variables. No 'hide and seek' game with incentive benefits at the end of the year. I wish to design my own compensation structure, please. ('Design your pay' is already followed by P&G, CTS.)

12) How is your work-life balance?

Very excellent! Unable to handle problems at home, I come early to office and leave very late. After going home, I start checking mails and act to be busy. Thus I balance work and personal life.

This is a sample as to how questions can be fielded and countered. With high dose of humour, you would have rolled on floor laughing.

Dear Interviewers, there are possibilities of a candidate answering in this fashion which you would have never come across. An interviewer does not know in what mood a candidate comes. Interviewer should ask questions in decent tone with maturity, utmost patience, dignity and calm state of mind. How else should an interviewer be? Interviewer shouldn't put questions and learn concepts from the candidate to brush up knowledge. The candidate is not here to teach.

English or Tamil or Hindi, whatever be the language spoken in the interview, should be free of grammar pitfalls and inadvertent use of words. He has to expose his personality skills in a better way and never should try to pull down the brand image of his employer. An interviewer should always appear in formal wear. (If dress code allows, casuals will be fine on weekends.) All etiquettes and manners discussed earlier for interviewees will hold good to interviewers also.

A candidate comes for the interview in response to your call. Respect him in all probable ways and accommodate him for at least ten minutes even if he does not have a chance to get selected. (Many interviewers reading this would mumble to say 'why then to waste time rather sending him out?) Before a candidate could come and occupy the seat, never force him out saying 'Thank you, we would let you know.'

Do not investigate into his personal matters and family feuds on the pretext of asking questions. Avoid stress test. (You are not going to send him to space station to test his stress and mental fatigue.) Repetitive irritating questions should be avoided for which answers cannot be reasonable. Certain answers had to be decently accepted and not to be argued about candidate's past destiny that was beyond his control. External pressing factors might have influenced him to change track and take up odd jobs.

By now you would have got a clear idea as to how an interviewer and interviewee should behave and follow the etiquettes of interview. To a candidate there are two people who are responsible for conveying the brand image. They are Front office Executive and HR Manager, who happen to meet them at first sight. At any cost these members should present a respectable status.

A recap of the interviewer code of business:

1.Greet the candidate with a smile and show enthusiasm

2.Make him feel comfortable and allow to settle down 3.Introduce yourself and establish a friendly atmosphere

4.Sincerely compliment good and favorable points in his CV

5.Keep a structured agenda of questions to ask

6.Ask open-ended questions - how, why, tell me, what, (and to a lesser extent where, when, which) to get into talking

7.If a position demands for profiling test or psychometric test, administer it and make the result available to him

8.Mind your tone, words, grammar and body language 9.Don't rush. Plan and make use of the time effectively

10. Once your turn is over, allow him to clarify his doubts

11. Close the interview on positive note with a smile Convey what is the next process and sign off

Chapter 12: How Long Were You In Your Last Job For?

From The Perspective Of The Candidate

Here again, employers want to separate out those who are unstable from those who are. If you are always leaving jobs within or up to a year, you are likely to be considered as very unstable. You need to understand the way employers think. Most of them take employees on, use about six or so months to teach them about their companies and how things are done, and remember they will be spending money on you all this time. So if you leave within another six months, they have just made a loss. Now, potential employers don't have a way of gauging how long you will stay with them except by looking at how long you have stayed in other places. If you are just seeking a job for the first time or you have left a few places in the past within one year, then you'll need to provide some assurance to the potential employer that you don't intend to leave their employment anytime soon. You can't just say "I'll be here for a while" – you have to let them see a reason why you intend to stay. Maybe you have a personal programme to gain as much experience from this particular employer that you can't find with any organisation (and don't try to flatter them, because they always know); maybe the organisation itself provides an excellent personnel development programme that you want to take full advantage of; maybe you are a family person and you need some stability in your career; maybe you have gained a great deal of experience in other places and now, you need to settle down; maybe they are the only organisation which provides the type of career you want to develop in; or maybe you have other past events in your life that you can use to prove that you are a very committed person (not your girlfriend/boyfriend type of commitment though). Whatever the case give the potential employer a reason to believe s/he won't be making a loss employing you.

From The Perspective Of The Employer

Employers will always draw a conclusion from this question by looking at two things; first, the frequency and second, the reason. If the candidate has left all their previous jobs in less than two years and mostly because of conflict with someone, then surely employers need to ask more questions because, all those people can't be so impossible to work with. It is also a question for which the employer is highly likely to request specific answers to his/her questions and not the general well-known answers such as; "I was looking for better opportunities" – well then, what opportunities were you looking for that your former employer didn't provide?

WHY DO YOU WANT TO WORK FOR THIS ORGANISATION?

From The Perspective Of The Candidate

STOP! Don't open your mouth if what you are about to say is very generic. For example, things like because you treat your staff well, because you are the leader in the industry; because you are the biggest company. STOP IT! This is the one question that shows clearly, which candidates have thoroughly researched the organisation BUT most importantly who know by themselves whether this is the right company for them or not.

Here is what you should also know – this question is also an opportunity for you to demonstrate to your employer that you are different from everybody else, because the truth is – everybody else is likely to be giving those same generic answers. What the employer is trying to establish with this question is whether or not the organisation also satisfies any of your needs or expectations. This is based on the understanding that no two people can agree to be together, and be successful in doing, except if they are satisfied with each other – in other words, the organisation must be happy that you'll satisfy its expectations and you, on the other hand must also be satisfied that the organisation will satisfy your expectations. Most jobseekers don't recognise the latter, but it is very true.

So how do you prepare for this kind of question? Make a list of the things that would make any job, your most satisfying job (I said satisfying NOT perfect) Also list down your future career plans, professional plans, development plans, personal plans that are closely related to your career. Now, find out by researching, if there are things about and within the organisation that will satisfy the needs and expectations you listed. I'm hoping you wouldn't see this as just a step to getting a job but it should also help you determine whether this is an employment you will be happy in or not. If anything about the organisation (now or its future) conflicts in a major way with your current or future plans, think twice.

From The Perspective Of The Employer

This question helps the employer pick up a few things. Firstly whether the candidate, by his or herself has assessed the culture of the organisation as matching their personal culture, and the reason the candidate really wants to be there. It will also tell you whether they have done any work in trying to understand the organisation or if they are just looking for somewhere to work for now. By asking this question the employer will also be able to find out the areas and parameters on which the candidates feel connected to the organisation? If any of those parameters happen to be the organisation's top cultures or values or principles, then, with some degree of certainty, the candidate will feel more at home there.

Chapter 13: Top Job Interview Questions

How do you react to negative feedback, especially from your superiors at work?

Everyone has moments where they disagree with their supervisors, and some of these people verbalize it. This question could be a trap for anyone on the receiving end, as there are risks to every type of answer. If you choose to play it safe, and tell your interviewer that the situation has never yet come up, you may just be signaling to them that you are a yes-man, someone who has no spine, and someone who may not end up contributing in any meaningful way. On the other hand, if you do speak about such an occurrence, there may be a chance that you will sound like you are speaking out of spite, something that may immediately turn off the interviewer. You may even speak about such occurrences casually, thinking that for you, things like these mean little as you are independent and opinionated. To an interviewer, however, you will likely look like a potential troublemaker.

It is possible to make yourself look good when answering this question, however. First, if ever such a situation happens to you, try to see whether or not the problem was due to miscommunication. Many problems at work are often due to that simple issue, miscommunication. If it wasn't simply miscommunication, then try to understand the root cause of the disagreement. What would their perception of the disagreement be? Why do they see it that way? If ever the problem does lie on your end, make sure to own up to it and remember to learn from it in order to not repeat the mistake. If you are able to handle issues like that, simply tell the interviewer what happened, and they will see that you were able to be mature, tried your best to understand the other person's position, and learned from the situation that came up. However, there is a possibility that something really hasn't come up, perhaps due to proper communication, or simply that you do not yet have much work experience. If so, be honest, but try to give the interviewer more information to work with, such as how you would react in such a situation. Talk about how you value proper communication, how you would sort out misunderstandings, and how you would own up to it if ever the mistake was on your end. This allows you to show your interviewer how you would be as an employee and co-worker, and shows that you are able to readily handle prickly situations such as your boss disagreeing with you. Remember that you should never lie in an interview, especially since people have an instinct for detecting lies, and the one interviewing you probably has a lot of experience with fact-checking, as well as a good eye for discovering falsehoods. What you don't want to happen is your interviewer mistrusting you through instinct. At the end of the day, just be honest, and make sure to impress on them the fact that if ever you made a mistake, it was a one-time thing, and it was a learning experience for you. Doing so will help smooth over any doubts your interviewer may have about you.

How motivated are you to carry out this role?

This type of question is usually directed to those with a few more years on them. Older people tend to run into problems when looking for new jobs, as they are often thought to be outdated, especially when it comes to new technology. Other people also feel that they are not as flexible as younger job-seekers, and they may not be amenable to working under a younger supervisor. Another concern often held by interviewers is the simple question of whether or not they still have energy and motivation to do well in the job, and if they still have the ambition to aim higher. That's the main concern that you have to address when answering the question of your motivation. There are several ways to answer it, the first one being to take it head on. You can acknowledge that there is a certain element of risk when hiring someone who is older, but you can also talk about the advantage that your work experience means that they have references available to them, references who will vouch for your competence and effectiveness. Of course, if you do choose to take this route, make sure to choose the most favorable references to you, especially former bosses who you worked well with. Remember to remind them that they may be called by the interviewer, and tell them what aspects of your work would be the best to talk about. The second way to answer this question is to refer more directly to your experience and accomplishments, preferably recent ones, to show the interviewer that you've still got what it takes to succeed. The third way seems flippant, but may be effective. If the interviewer is around your age as well, you can simply say: "Well, do you still have the drive to succeed? I haven't lost mine." This is risky, as the interviewer may take offense, but if they see you as similar to them, that's a plus for you. The fourth and last suggestion that we can offer, is to simply prepare. You can simply acknowledge that you are old, but show them you are still motivated by talking about your plans, maybe even drawing out a thirty-sixty-ninety day plan that you prepared in advance. If you do have one ready, that is one of the most unquestionable ways to show you still have the drive to succeed, as you took the time and effort to prepare, showing them just how much you value the job prospect, and how important doing well in it means to you.

What is your method of transacting with problematic clients?

Regrettably, people in the service industry have to face problematic people every now and again. No matter what your job is, whether you are a clerk, a waiter/waitress, a service representative, or any other role in the service industry, you will eventually run into a client who just refuses to cooperate, or is rude, or is any one of a number of things that makes them difficult to deal with. Those in the service industry are representative of the company, as they are the ones that clients deal with daily, in the front line. Therefore, how people in the service sector act may greatly affect the public perception of the company, which plays a large role in a company's revenue. If ever your interviewer asks this question, you have to show them that you understand the importance of your job, and your answer should be tailored towards that point. One of the better ways to do this is to simply tell them a story of how you successfully dealt with a problematic client, and if you have a reference or a note from your supervisor at the time, or even the customer concerned, then even better. Direct evidence of effectiveness will ensure that you have this question in the bag. However, the most important thing to show when answering the question is how you look at the service industry in general, and what your philosophy is when dealing with customers. One answer that encapsulates a desirable outlook is: "When I deal with problematic clients, I have the same mentality as I do when I deal with cooperative ones. I want to ensure that they have the best experience possible when transacting with the company. I won't give the client any reason to badmouth us or regret giving us our business, so if their concern is something I can fix, I will do my best to do so. If I can't fix it, I'll try to find a way to turn it into a positive experience: perhaps give them a refund, or some other product or service in order to keep them happy. I treat every client like I would a close friend." This type of answer shows how you look at clients and how you see your responsibility of dealing with them. It shows the interviewer that you will do everything you can to give clients a good experience, and you will defend the good image of the company with your actions. This answer also shows that you take responsibility even for difficult clients, rather than simply passing them on to a co-worker, or a supervisor. Highlighting those qualities effectively will most likely lead to you becoming a shoo-in for the job.

How do you react when confronted with a difficult situation?

If your interviewer asks how you deal with difficult situations, there is a high chance that you'd want to make an off-the-cuff joke referencing the job interview you are currently undergoing. After all, no matter how composed we are on the outside, or how experienced we are with undergoing interviews, it is only natural to have some nerves when at the interview itself. Much as we'd like to make a flippant comment to allow ourselves to relax, a job interview is not the best time to make a joke like that. The question itself is a standard interview questions, as everyone in the world gets stressed at some point. Eventually we come face-to-face with a difficult situation, and the interviewer wants to make sure that we are able to compose ourselves and face the situation head-on, rather than throwing a tantrum, running away, or any other alienating and fruitless response. When they ask this question, they are in fact inviting you to tell them about your experience in dealing with a difficult, stressful occurrence, and they are waiting to see how you fared. Remember when you tell a story, follow the STAR framework. This framework simply means Situation/Task, Action, and Result. This allows you to keep on track and minimize rambling, allowing you to get your point across. Remember that this question is during a job interview, so it is best to respond by telling a work story, and how you dealt with a work-related incident. Some of the best traits to emphasize when telling a story are how you maintained composure, and your methods of solving problems. One example of a problem-solving method is breaking down the initial problem into smaller, more easily solvable problems. Breaking them down in this manner shows that you are methodical and thorough when dealing with any issues that come up. At the end of the day, the most important thing is that you are able to show your prospective employer that you are productive and take initiative when solving problems, rather than backing down or handing them off to other people.

What is success to you?

When you hear this question from the interviewer, remember the context that you are in. Your interviewer is not asking for a philosophical take on success, and neither do they need to know what you consider to be a successful life in general. If you try to talk to them about success as an abstract context, you'll probably be out of the running. When they ask about success, they are asking about success in the job, not about whether or not having a happy relationship can be considered as success, or if retiring to the beach is your vision of success. Job interviews are basically sales. You are selling yourself, the product, to the interviewer, who is your customer. As your customer, he is asking what a successful product looks like, meaning how you will consider success in the context of work. Remember to do your research on the company you're interviewing for, and prep accordingly. You should know what they need, and you should be carrying the conversation based on how your product is the best product for their particular set of needs. In this case, success may be best defined as achieving goals that have been set, achieving them in the best and most efficient manner possible, and being able to make your bosses happy in the process. Telling them as well that success to you is being able to finish a project promptly, within budget, and to the satisfaction of the project's customer is another way to make the interviewer happy. If you happen to be interviewing for a managerial or executive position, success could be defined as getting those under you to work smoothly and effectively, setting a profitable direction for your division, or any number of things that reflect on what you want your goals to be in that position. One tip that may prove to be helpful is, after defining success, you can ask the interviewer what they consider success at the company, and you can use the information you get from their response to improve your answers for the next questions in the interview.

How do you deal with work-related stress?

People react to difficult situations in different manners. Some people complain, some people run away from their problems, and some people take it out on others. Other people use stress as a motivator to do better, and others simply ignore it and carry on as usual. Of course, companies would be enthused to have employees of the latter two types. Therefore, everyone answers that they thrive on pressure, or they are able to remain composed under stress. Interviewers already expect this, and answering like that has already become similar to answering "I am never satisfied with good enough" to: "what would you say your weakness is?" Of course, if your reaction to pressure is really to work harder and do well, then be honest about it. After all, there truly are people who operate that way, and if you are one of them, your interviewer will likely detect the sincerity in your answer. If you are also the type of person who simply breathes deeply and continues to focus on what they have to do, then say so. Similarly, if you really are like that, then the interviewer will most likely realize that you are simply being honest. If you are neither, there is no shame in it, but you have to think more about what to answer. This question requires an honest answer, but it also necessitates that you show the interviewer that you are still effective even if stressed. You can explain your coping mechanisms, such as breaking big tasks into little, more easily solvable ones in order to make it look easier to deal with. You could talk about how you choose to prioritize when you are bombarded with tasks and responsibilities. Almost every job has an element of stress baked in, and at some point in your career, you will have to deal with stress. What the interviewer needs to know is that you are able to deal with it in a positive manner and remain productive. Remember that when you talk about your methods for dealing with stress, talking about a work-related story helps illustrate the point and allows them to better understand the qualities that you wish to tell them about.

If you were to give yourself a rating, what would it be?

When it comes to this question and others like it, some people believe that the best policy is extreme confidence, to the point of giving yourself an eleven over ten. They think that any other answer is tantamount to undermining yourself in the eyes of the interviewer. However, if you think about it, giving an overconfident answer like that is simply bragging, and nobody likes a braggart. During an interview, you should be selling yourself, and being overconfident to the point of arrogance would not inspire any enthusiasm in a hiring manager. Be realistic when you rate yourself, but of course try to paint yourself in a beneficial light. If the scale is over ten, then perhaps a score somewhere within the range of six to eight would be a reasonable answer. If you have no experience yet, for example, perhaps a fresh graduate, then six or seven is not unreasonable. The only time you should ever give yourself a score as high as ten is if you truly are an expert in that field, and you have the credentials to back it up. Once you've given an honest, realistic rating, explain your reasoning to them. For example, if you rate yourself a six or six point five over ten, say that for you, five is the average and you feel that you are better than average, but you have much to learn. Remember to back your reasoning up with evidence that justifies it, or the interviewer may think you are simply blustering. It's always helpful to identify a few things that set you apart from other applicants, things that you know prospective employers look for. If you are able to answer this question with a sincere and well-justified answer, you will look very good in the eyes of the hiring manager.

Chapter 14: Sell Yourself: Developing The Right Communication Skills

Here are 10 communication techniques to master, each is just as important in personal and social life, as well as at work or outside the office with your colleagues. By learning these techniques by heart, you will be able to quickly connect to anyone, earn their respect, and gain influence.

BE FRIENDLY. People are drawn to signs of friendliness. People with a smiling face and pleasing personality always have an edge in every communication. Friendly people bring an automatic wave of calmness; they put people at ease, enabling them to open up and speak freely. This is a must, especially when your aim is to practice your communication skills. People who are ready to listen and share will make everything easier for any speaker.

NEVER SOUND LIKE A FOOL. Think before you speak. Be prudent enough to think first before talking about something. People who never filter their words are often considered reckless. It is important to always know what you are talking about. And even if you know what you are talking about, make sure that you are sensitive enough to tell if what you are saying will produce a negative reaction among your listeners. People with good communication skills often leave their listeners inspired and feeling great.

CLEAR AS CRYSTAL. If you want to excel in communication, find ways to convey your message in a brief and clear manner. Avoid being indirect as it would only confuse your listeners. You would not want to leave your audience bewildered and asking what it was you really meant.

TOO MUCH IS ALWAYS BAD. Be concise, less is always good when conveying your message. Never attempt to sound "intellectual" by injecting too many words. Also, never use jargons and difficult words just to project an impressive image. No matter how many words you use, how many sentences, if your listeners are not able to absorb what you are saying, then you fail as a speaker.

BE AUTHENTIC. Integrity, humility, and honesty are very important when conveying something. People have the natural ability to detect inconsistencies in what others are saying, so never pretend just to win over your listeners.

BE CONFIDENT. Humility is never about the lack of confidence. On the other hand, humility is about knowing what you are capable of and knowing your limitations. The self-awareness you get from humility should be enough to boost your confidence. Speak with a conviction that you know what you are saying; use appropriate tone to convince them of your honesty and sincerity. Make eye contact to draw them to you and the things you want to say to them.

BODY LANGUAGE. Your body language plays a significant role in relaying your messages. Hand gestures and facial expressions will always make it easier for your listeners to understand what you are saying. So, use them to your advantage and eliminate the chances of being misunderstood. Your body language will put real meaning to the words you are using.

TONE IS EVERYTHING. Whether you are face to face with someone or you are speaking to somebody over the phone, your tone plays a big part in perfecting your communication skills. Words are naked without the proper tone. Tone gives your words the authority they need to be absorbed by your listeners. Over the phone, tone dresses you up in the mind of the listener.

POSITIVE SCRIPTING. Words are powerful. With the right vocabulary and the right tone, you can make other people feel better. Practice using positive words in conveying your thoughts and emotions even when telling something about a challenging experience. In doing so, people around you will always feel happy when with you.

LISTEN. It is only natural to be drawn to someone who is a great listener. Even when you are not connecting with anyone, people will remember you if you take this technique by heart, they may even contact you when they need to talk to someone. It will be a huge compliment on your part when someone contacts you and invite you for a quick chat. This shall be a clear sign that you are moving forward in your quest to acquire good communication skills.

Follow these techniques and you will never go wrong. When your listeners are able to feel good when talking to you, they will open up to you more and share. In return, they themselves can make your job as the speaker a lot easier. The aim of the techniques above is to make sure that you always establish a good rapport with your listeners. With enough practice, you will find out that your very positive presence is enough to draw people around you.

Chapter 15: Common Interview Questions And Their Best

In general, the questions asked by the interviewers during the interview will focus on two aspects: your background and your skills. They will clarify and cross-check your resume and the answers you've provided in the application forms. The goal is to determine if the position is a good fit for you.

Nevertheless, sometimes the interviewers will ask other, out-of-context, questions too to test your character and personality. They will "intimidate" you, poke fun at you, and put you in a corner. Not infrequently, they will use good cop/bad cop tactics. The goal is to reveal your true personality.

The style and tone used by the interviewers vary too. Sometimes they will use a formal tone, but other times they will use an informal tone. Regardless of the style, you must always be formal, professional, and confident. Be humble, however, and avoid being overconfident.

In order not to fall into the interviewers' trap, always give a concise, straight-to-the-point answer. Don't get upset if they mock you and poke fun at you. Never talk negatively, especially about your previous roles and employers.

Avoid whining, complaining, or telling sad stories. Always give positive and optimistic answers. If they disagree with you about something or doubt your capability, explain to them logically and politely without showing your emotions or feelings. Show them that you are a capable, mature and reliable person.

For first-time job seekers and fresh graduates, the interview stage seems the most difficult. I have experienced this myself. However, as time passes and as you attend more interviews, your fears and anxiety will disappear. You may even laugh during an interview.

Lastly, I will tell you a little secret about job interviews. In the last 20 years, I have worked full-time, part-time, and freelance in the food, retail, IT, translation, advertising, and publishing companies as sales, cashier, technician, writer, translator, reporter, editor, and in other roles, and one thing that I have learned is that most job interview questions are the same!

What does this mean to you? You're right! You can learn and practice the interview before you actually go to one. And, that's not all. You can even prepare your answers beforehand!

Below are the list of common interview questions and their best answers. Prepare your answers carefully beforehand. Write them down on a piece of paper. Ask someone to do a mock interview with you.

1) Tell me about yourself. Here you are asked to provide basic background information about yourself, starts with your name, place and date of birth, school,

work experience, up to the present. For example, my name is George Walker. I was born in New York on January 8, 1995. I'm the fifth child out of six. My father is a high school teacher and my mom is a housewife. I'm an alumnus of Faculty of X of X State University class of 2017.

2) What were your roles and responsibilities in your previous job? Or, if you are a fresh graduate, what were the findings of your thesis? Tell them briefly about your daily duties in your previous job. Don't be too lengthy. Just cover the basic essentials. For fresh graduates, tell them about the theme of your thesis. Don't go into too much detail, just talk about the conclusions.

3) Why are you interested in this position? Tell them that you love the job. That it matches your interests and passion or your educational background (if it's the case). For example, if you apply for a sales position, tell them how you love selling and business. Or if you apply for a job as a teacher, tell them how you love teaching

and education. Show them that you are excited and very enthusiastic about working in that particular field.

4) What do you know about this position?

Tell them everything you know about the position. This is why it is important to do a research about the position before going to the interview.
5) What are your strengths? Identify your strengths that are relevant to the position that you are applying for. For example, if you are applying for a job as a reporter, tell them if you have excellent writing skills, and so on.

6) What is your greatest weakness? Find one weakness that is not relevant to, or even better, supports the position. For example, if you apply for a position that requires you to travel frequently and meet new people, tell them how you can't sit still for too long. Or if the position requires keen eye for detail, tell them that you're a perfectionist.
7) What is the most memorable event in

your life? Tell them about the happiest moment in your life. Choose a positive and constructive event when you ACHIEVE something good. For example, when you graduated from school or won a race or a competition. When they ask you why this was your most memorable event, tell them that after all the effort you put in, you finally made it.

8) What is the saddest experience in your life? NEVER, ever, tell something personal here, such as your love or family life :D Instead, pick a neutral event. For example, when you're looking for a job and fail to get one. You're sad because you cannot use your skills or you cannot make your parents or your loved ones happy.

9) What did you do to overcome it? Tell them how you worked hard to improve your skills and continue with your job search.

10) What is your favorite job? The answer to this question is easy. Tell them it's the job that you are applying for. When they

ask you the reason, tell them all the positive things about the job and how your interest, skills and experience relate to the position.

11) What job did you dislike most? Pick a job that is the opposite of the position you are applying for. If the position requires you to be active such as sales or reporter, pick opposite jobs such as teacher or clerk. If they ask you why, tell them the nature of the job was contrary to the position you're applying for.

12) Why should we hire you? Tell them that you are very interested in the position. And that you are confident that you can do the job because it matches your skills, experience or educational background (if that's the case). If you have no relevant experience, tell them that you are a fast learner and you fully understand the job scope. Remember, this is only a test. You may boast a little here.

13) Tell me about your family? What values your family taught you? Tell them

about your family, starting with your parents and siblings. Keep it brief. Just tell them about their education and jobs. Tell them how your parents taught you about honesty, integrity, hard work and so on.

14) What do you do in your spare time? Or what are your hobbies? Give a positive answer such as reading, writing, photography, and so forth.In general, a company wants an active, happy, sociable employee with good communication skills. They don't like quiet, individualistic, and moody employees.

15) What do you want to do in your life? Where do you see yourself five years from now. Give an answer that is in line with the position. For example, if you're applying for a job as a reporter, tell them that you want to be an editor five years from now. Likewise, if you're applying to be a teacher, tell them that you want to be a school principal in five years.

16) Why did you quit your last job? NEVER, ever, utter negative comments about your

former job, including your former boss. Give a neutral and positive answer, such as to advance your career, to pursue better opportunities, and so on.

17) What is your expected salary? For fresh graduates, it would be safer not to state a nominal value here. Remember, this is only a test to find out how much you value yourself or how logical are you! They already have a salary scale.

So, tell them that you expect a salary that is in line with the company's policy and industry standards and commensurate with your qualifications and experience.

If they tell you that the salary for the position is low, tell them that you have total confidence in the company's policy and that the company must already have its own salary policy (NB. You can turn down the offer later after the initial interview if the salary is actually lower than you expect).

MORE INTERVIEW TIPS

To ace the interview stage, try noting these questions along with their answers on a piece of paper or in your smartphone. Ask a friend or family to conduct a mock job interview.

Read the questions and answers out loud. Keep practicing this every day. Try to get used to the questions and answers. The more you practice, the more familiar you'll be with the questions and answers and the better the results. Happy job hunting and good luck!

Chapter 16: Pre-Interview Preparation: Professional Standards

Alongside the obvious ways in which you must prepare for a job search and interview—resume, cover letter, research, practice—you also have to consider the professional standards that are being asked of you in any given professional scenario. The research that you have conducted on the company should give you some sense of the standards of professionalism that the company will require—a tech start-up and an investment banker position will probably vary widely in what they expect. Nevertheless, it is always better, especially in an application and interview scenario, to err on the side of **more** professional rather than less. Professional etiquette is shown in how you present yourself, from the way you are groomed and dressed to the way in which you greet people and respond.

Some General Guidelines for Professional Etiquette

Certainly, any good job interview begins with an idea first impression, and that first impression is informed by how we look, particularly, how we are dressed and groomed prior to the interview. In recent years, the standards for what constitutes "business" dress have been changed and, for the most part, expanded. Still, a job interview is more than likely more formal than typical employee dress standards (especially when considering the proliferation of "casual Fridays" and tech start-ups jeans and t-shirts). Whatever the company for which you are interviewing, you should follow some basic guidelines to ensure that you are looking professional and making a smart first impression.

Looking Professional

In doing your company research, you should have some broader knowledge of company culture, including how employees are supposed to present themselves in the workplace. Use that knowledge to base your understanding of how to present yourself at an interview: as stated above, an interview is likely a more formal affair than an everyday work look, but it gives you a starting point. Be sure to peruse any company photos, especially on social media, to get an idea of how employees dress when they are representing the company.

While you are trying to look your best—professional and poised—you should also take into consideration your comfort level. That is, don't wear something that is too tight, too bulky, or too warm to an interview. The more comfortable you are in your professional attire, the more confidence you project. Be sure to take the seasons into the occasion, and wear layers if you tend to get warm during an interview; you can take off a jacket should you need to, if you are wearing a nice dress shirt or blouse underneath.

Avoid wearing anything that is revealing, such as a sundress or low-cut blouse. This guideline doesn't at first appear to relate to men, but a vee-necked shirt or lack of socks might fall along these lines for men. The idea is not to look like you're going out with friends, but they are representing yourself professionally for a company.

Be certain that your clothes are recently cleaned, especially if you plan to wear a suit or other truly formal attire, and check for stains, tears, or other signs of distress. If you do not have an appropriate outfit for an interview and lack the financial ability to purchase one quickly, there are many resources in communities, like Dress for Success, that will help you find something appropriate at a reasonable price—or for free.

Lay or set out your clothes the night before the interview. This ensures that you make a good inspection of everything (if you have pets, be sure to give yourself a quick roll before you leave the house) and that you don't have any last-minute delays. One of the worst things you can do is to show up late for an interview: give yourself plenty of time to get ready and to get there on time.

Finally, don't second guess yourself or overthink it. If you feel reasonably comfortable and have chosen a clean, pressed outfit that seems to meet the standards of the company, then you are probably going to be just fine.

Special Considerations for Men:

In nearly every case of interviewing for a traditional company, a suit is required, regardless of standards for the everyday dress as an employee. Again, do your research, but always err on the side of being conservative when in doubt.

According to most experts, a dark suit with a light-colored shirt is the most standard suit attire. Be sure that you have a matching tie, coordinated socks, and a nice belt, in addition.

Again, if you do not own a suit, now is the time to invest in one—one that fits and is comfortable, not something that you had leftover from a cousin's wedding ten years ago. If you need assistance financially with acquiring a suit, check into local organizations that help people find employment.

Beware of loud colors or overbearing ties; certainly, you want to avoid anything that seems overly whimsical or novelty (this is not the time to wear cartoon- or NFL-patterned ties).

Of course, you want to appear neat and clean, but also be aware to avoid strong colognes or other scents; you do not want to trigger a reaction in an interviewer. Check your nails, too, as your hands will be noticed during an interview, from your handshake to handing out of documents and such.

Avoid smoking before the interview, if at all possible. You don't want to bring in lingering smells of tobacco or other odors that might be unpleasant to an interviewer.

Groom your hair nicely. Again, the rules

for how to wear one's hair have changed dramatically over the last couple of decades, especially for men. Use your best judgment and follow what you see on the company's web site as a guide. An investment banking company will probably want to see short, conservative hair, while a tech start-up will likely not be bothered by longer or different styles.

If you are called for a second interview, the best rule of thumb is to dress like your potential employer; this could mean being slightly less formal, but not always. At that point, you should have a good feel for the company in order to understand and integrate the culture.

Special Considerations for Women:

Some of the same rules apply to women: you should probably wear some kind of suit, either with a skirt or pants. When wearing a skirt to an interview, you should always wear some kind of hose rather than presenting bare legs. Typically, you should avoid open-toed shoes or sandals.

Again, do your research and peruse pictures of employees on social media. When in doubt, be more conservative than not.

Remember to make sure that you are comfortable, and practice seeing how you feel when you are sitting down; an ill-fitting jacket has a tendency to gap when you are seated, and a tight waistband on pants or a skirt will cause discomfort. Most stores offer some sort of minor tailoring to have adjustments made to what you might purchase for an interview.

If your budget doesn't allow you to purchase something nice for the interview, seek out local organizations that assist people in gaining employment. There are places that will help you find something appropriate, like the Dress for Success program.

As with the advice for men, wear something that is darker in color, avoiding bright or flashy colors and embellishments, for the most part. A dark suit with a lighter blouse is considered the standard. Never wear low-cut blouses or sheer fabrics of any kind, and make sure the length of your skirt, if wearing one, is appropriate. Conservative interviewers often complain about the length of skirts; too short is inappropriate, while too long isn't professional. Stick to roughly knee-length skirts for interview occasions.

If you must accessorize, then be judicious: don't cover your hands in rings or wear stacks of bracelets or long, chunky necklaces and earrings. Accessories are your chance to shine, really, if you employ them properly. With a conservative suit, one nice pendant or pair of pretty earrings can really pop and make you stand out.

The same ideas above also apply to hair and make-up: be relatively conservative. Don't wear heavy eye make-up or drastically dark lipstick; these looks aren't considered wholly professional. With hair, keep it neat and tidy—be yourself, of course—and avoid overly stylized or trendy looks (such as lavender hair or faux beehive dos). Nails should be groomed, but avoid long, overly decorated nails, especially of the trendy press-on type. Not only do these appear flashy and lack professionalism, but they get in the way of your ability to execute daily business tasks.

When it comes to shoes, avoid the kind of shoe you'd wear out on the weekend. Keep the heel to a minimum, and be sure that the shoes are closed both at the toe and the back. A basic pump style is always available, and these comfortable yet smart shoes will virtually never go out of style. It's a good one-time investment in a neutral color, such as brown or black.

Match your hose to your skin color, rather than wearing colorful or graphically printed tights. Remember that the goal is to draw attention to your skills, not your style.

Obviously, you want to be neat and clean for the interview, and be sure to avoid heavy perfumes or other scents that may be overpowering for others in an interview. Don't smoke right before the interview; if you can avoid it, smelling of smoke can be a negative trigger for many. As with the advice above for men, the guidelines for what constitutes professional dress have shifted and broadened over the last couple of decades. This is why doing your research into the company is important for you to have a clear sense of what would be the most appropriate attire. Still, it is doubtless best to err on the side of caution rather than flamboyance for an interview.

If called for a second interview, follow the cues that you picked up while at first. Dress like your boss, perhaps a touch more conservatively, and you should be in line with what is expected.

Acting Professional

Acting professionally consists of any number of minor behaviors and skills of etiquette. As anyone who has worked with others in any capacity before well knows, the attitude one displays and the behavior one engages in speaks volumes about personal character and professional capacity. When embarking on an interview, it is understandable to be intimated by strangers who have some sort of control over your potential future. However, now that you have snagged the interview with your sharp resume and descriptive cover letter, you need only to look—and act—the part. The following tips should help you develop your professional etiquette for the interview. See the next chapter for some other tips on how to put your best foot forward for any job scenario.

Remember that one of the crucial tests you must pass when attending a job interview is the litmus test of whether you will fit into the culture of the company. In general terms, this means that you need to demonstrate professional etiquette and respect not only to your interviewer but toward anyone else you may encounter (other employees, like a receptionist or secretary or colleagues in your department or group). Your skills are rendered irrelevant if your behavior is boorish and rude. Consider your first impression; you must not only look the part but also act the part. A first impression can never be retracted, so it is important not to begin an interview on the wrong foot. From the moment you arrive at the company, be on your most professional behavior: for all you know, the person you greet in the hallway or ride in the elevator with maybe your future boss or colleague. Be enthusiastic and look happy—rather than apprehensive—to be there. Make eye contact and introduce yourself politely when appropriate, extending a handshake in most cases. When entering the interview space, be sure to accept instructions politely and strike and open—rather than defensive—posture.

As mentioned above, be sure that the outfit you've chosen to wear for the interview is appropriate and professional, but also be aware of how it will appear when you are seated. You want to avoid the proverbial wardrobe malfunction (gaping blouse, popped button, overly hiked pants). Typically, you will be seated for most of the interview, so that's how you should test the comforts and utility of your chosen attire. Always remember to smile and appear interested in what the interviewer is saying. A smile (or, conversely, a frown) can speak volumes. If you appear smiling and approachable, then you are perceived as a team player with valuable character attributes as well as professional skills to bring to the company. A frown, on the other hand, can fluster or annoy the interviewer; it is difficult to know how to interpret the facial expression. Are you angry, annoyed, bored, frustrated, or otherwise unimpressed? This is not the impression you want to convey. Remind yourself that this experience, while somewhat nerve-racking, should be an amicable way in which to showcase your considerable talents and value. This would bring a smile to anyone's face.

Body language, in general, reveals a lot about a person's feelings and character. Crossing your arms against your chest looks defensive, even hostile, while a lazy slump indicates a lack of interest or disrespect. Keeping your hands folded in your lap throughout the interview can have the effect of implying childlike anxiety. "Man-spreading" can look aggressive or arrogant. Again, maintain eye contact when answering questions and avoid sweeping hand gestures. You can hold a pen or pencil in your hand if it helps to center you, and this can come in handy should you wish to jot anything down. Basically, your body language should indicate that you are engaged and open, enthusiastic, and polite.

When greeting others, be sure that you have a solid handshake, somewhere between limp and crushing. A firm handshake reveals self-confidence and a courteous understanding of overall business etiquette. When meeting someone for the first time, it is considered polite to use an honorific, such as Dr. or Ms. or Mr. If the company for which you are interviewed is owned or operated by foreign nationals, then it would behoove you to do some research into the basic etiquette of the other country. Personal space is defined differently in different cultures, in addition to attitudes about how men and women behave.

Addressing someone by their name is also a powerful piece of business etiquette that you can employ to curry respect. Everyone likes to be noticed and remembered, so try your best to remember and repeat the names of people that you meet. Should you be called in for a further interview, this considerate formality will inevitably be noticed. Still, don't sound sycophantic: continuously repeating the interviewer's name throughout the interview—"now, that's an interesting question, Dr. Jones. Let me see how I can answer that fully, Dr. Jones. Thank you, Dr. Jones"—can be annoying and patronizing.

As you are seated for your interview—which you should be invited to do, rather than simply plopping down—place your personal items beside or underneath your chair. For everyone's sanity and to preserve your dignity, turn off your cell phone and any other device you may have carried with you. Have your resume and cover letter, along with a notepad or folder for notes, at the ready.

If, for some disastrous reason, your phone should ring during an interview, you will be called upon to do some swift damage control. Do not dare look at the phone to check (unless you truly have a life-and-death situation on your hands); simply turn it off and apologize to the interviewer. You would have to be an excellent candidate to overcome this most egregious of etiquette breaches. It's better not to take your phone in with you if you have a habit of forgetting to switch it off. And off means **off**, not silent.

When leaving the interview, be sure to restate your interest in the job and your pleasure at having met everyone. Shake hands again and repeat names, when appropriate. Be sure to thank the receptionist who showed you in, if relevant. Basically, just show proper manners on your way out the door.

After the interview, it is customary to write a "thank you" note of some sort to the interviewer or interviewers to acknowledge their time and your opportunity. More on that will be covered in Chapter 12.

Chapter 17: Working With Staffing Companies

Just as a carpenter uses many tools to build a bookshelf, you'll probably need many tools to build your dream career. One tool to consider is the staffing company, also sometimes called recruiting agencies, headhunters, and employment agencies. No matter what you call them, though, they all have the same purpose: to connect employers with employees. Whether you've been struggling through a job search for months or are fresh to the job hunt, it is highly possible that one of these agencies can help you.

Staffing companies come in two main varieties: the temp agency and the recruiting firm. The former finds job seekers short-term positions, which can be great for High Priority job seekers, while the latter places job seekers into full-time careers. Both types have benefits and drawbacks, however, and not every agency is created equal — so be sure you are thoroughly familiar with the company's policies and reputation before signing up.

Staffing Agencies — Temporary

When businesses need short-term workers, they'll sometimes turn to temp agencies. These agencies sign on job seekers, and then select employees from a pool of candidates to send to employers. The length of time the employee works for each company varies widely, with some jobs lasting a few days and some a few months. The type of work also varies, from secretarial to warehouse to retail.

To determine which work would be the best fit for a candidate, most temp agencies submit job seekers to a range of tests, such as typing tests, and questionnaires. Job seekers who sign with temp agencies usually also have to sign an agreement that outlines the rules they are to follow regarding their employment. It is often forbidden for temp agency employees, for example, to discuss with their employer's being hired for full-time positions. This does not mean some temporary positions do not turn into full-time jobs, but usually the employer must first speak to the temp agency, not the employee.

If your job search is High Priority, especially if you are not currently employed, you might turn to a temp agency sooner rather than later. Besides the extra income this action will generate; the reasons for doing so are twofold. First, it is easier to get a job when you have a job, since employers see that you are employable. Second, signing on with a temp agency will help you prevent gaps in your resume, which are notoriously disliked by those in charge of hiring.

Benefits of Finding Jobs Through Temp Agencies:

-An employer may offer you a full-time position if you perform well and demonstrate professionalism.

-If you are not quite sure what your dream career is, you can experience several types of careers by working with a temp agency. As you take on a range of assignments, you can cross off the fields you do not enjoy and further explore those you do.

-By working a range of assignments, you'll be developing skills to add to your resume.

-Pursing temporary positions while you are looking for a job demonstrates commitment and a desire to remain employed — something that employer's value highly.

-You may not be offered a job, but you'll be meeting many new individuals who may be able to help you in the future.

Drawbacks of Finding Jobs Through Temp Agencies:

-Temporary positions often don't offer insurance, retirement plans, or other benefits, so you may need to find your own.

-Sometimes you may be assigned to a job in a field you are not interested in or don't find fulfilling.

-Your work is, by definition, temporary, which means you may have to weather short spells without any work.

-You might find you are working for less money than you feel you are worth, especially if you have a college degree or experience.

-Because the rest of the staff knows you are only working with them temporarily, it can sometimes be more difficult to forge deep connections.

Staffing Agencies — Non-Temporary

Job seekers who are in the Medium or Low Priority categories and who have jobs already might opt for an employment agency instead of a temp agency. These firms place job seekers with employers on a full-time basis, generally within the field the candidate is trained in, studied, or has experience in. Note, though, that recruiters, headhunters, and employment agencies are paid when they've made a placement, so they may sometimes offer job seekers positions that aren't a good fit in order to hit a quota.

Employment agencies can be divided into two categories depending on who initiates the relationship. On one side are the agencies that actively seek and recruit individuals to fill jobs for their clients, the employers. On the other side are the agencies that wait for job seekers to contact them. If you are looking for a job, it is probable that you'll deal with the latter. In this situation, you'll approach the agency; give them your resume; tell them about yourself, including your skills, training, and career goals; and be matched with potential employers. As with searching for a job on your own, you'll still need patience. The hiring market fluctuates, and the agency may or may not have a match for you immediately.

Before you jump into working with an employment agency, you should be clear on how its fees work. Most reputable firms do not charge the job seeker, so if you are asked to pay a fee upfront, you should view that as a red flag. Instead, it is a company the firm works for that pays them, which occurs in two different ways. Firms that work on a contingency are only paid after they've made a placement, which is usually calculated as a percentage of the amount you'll be paid. Firms that work on retainer, on the other hand, are paid a fixed fee upfront. Both can find you a job, but experts suggest working with firms that are on retainer, if only because they generally enjoy exclusivity with the companies they work for. Companies that have paid an agency up front are often more decisive in the hiring process, since they are not shopping around for candidates with many agencies. You'll also enjoy less competition.

Benefits of Finding Jobs Through Employment Agencies:

-These agencies often place candidates in jobs that will never be advertised — which means there's no other way to find them.

-Employment agencies find positions for people in all types of industries, so if your line of work is not in a large field, they still may have opportunities for you.

-You'll save time since working with an employment agency is essentially like having someone work for you.

Drawbacks of Finding Jobs Through Employment Agencies:

-Bachelor of Arts in Headhunting does not exist, so you'll need to check the qualifications of the individuals or firms you are working with carefully. Individuals who have backgrounds in human resources or related fields, or ones who have been in the business a long time, are probably more trustworthy.

-Most employment agencies are general, meaning they may not have insight into your particular field. You should perform your research before accepting job interviews to ensure that the position you are applying for is truly a good fit for your skills.

-Receiving little to no feedback from an employment agency is not unusual, which can be frustrating if you are trying to hone your job hunting and interviewing skills.

Chapter 18: Warning Signs To Look Out For During Your Interview

The interviewer bad mouths the company's competitors

If your interviewer can't wait to talk about their competition down, then alarm bells should be sounding for you. Quite apart from the fact that no-one wants to spend their days with someone who likes to be negative, ask yourself why your interviewer feels the need to do that.

Could it be that the competition is way ahead of the company you are interviewing for? Is the company perhaps in trouble because they can't keep up with their competitors? Or maybe the company is losing staff to the competition because they offer better pay or working conditions. Either way, listen carefully for clues in what the interviewer is saying – why not give the game a look and see what they can offer?

The interviewer bad mouths the person you are replacing

Interviewers should be professional, and they should know that their job is just as much about selling their company to you as it is about assessing you for a role.

If the interviewer is bad-mouthing the person who just left the role you are applying for, the chances are that something went very wrong with that working relationship, and you don't need that sort of atmosphere when you spend so much of your time at work.

You also don't know what the company will say about you behind your back or when you are leaving.

The interviewer can't demonstrate career progression

One of the most obvious questions to ask at an interview is about career progression, and you should, of course, ask this because you want to know, but this question can also give you an insight into the company you are applying for.

If the interviewer tries to fob you off, is unable to come up with recent, solid examples of how others have progressed within the company, or is unable to talk to you about a clear career path, it could be time to consider a quick exit.

The interviewer doesn't ever mention their team

One of the best things about a perfect job is working with a great team that supports each other, builds each other up, and stays positive no matter what. If your interviewer spends their time talking only about themselves, and the team barely gets a mention, you've got to wonder whether they're a team player and if everyone in the business is the same.

The interviewer can't explain to you why they enjoy working for the business

If you enjoy something, whether it's a film, the last date you had or your job, you can't wait to tell people about it, can you?

If your interviewer is barely able to scrape up a smile when you ask if they enjoy their job, it could be time to worry.

No one at the company looks happy in their role

While you're waiting in reception before your interview, look out for any other staff and see if they look happy at work. Is the receptionist genuinely pleasant and willing to chat with you? What is the interaction like between members of staff? Do they acknowledge you and try to make you feel welcome?

All of these things can help you decide whether this is the place for you.

The interviewer doesn't answer your questions

Evasion is never a good sign. If the interviewer tries to hustle you out of the door quickly and doesn't give you the chance to ask any questions, or even worse, if they actively avoid answering your questions, maybe there's something they are trying to hide.

The interviewer is vague about your role, the salary, and the benefits

If you can't get a clear picture of what you would be doing, or if the job description has markedly changed at the interview from what you applied for, those warning bells should be clanging again.

If you add to that no explicit discussion of the salary and benefits you can expect, it is time to head for the door!

Taking the time to think about what you want from the company you work for, watching for any warning signs, and listening to your gut in an interview situation can help you get a clearer picture of what it's like to work for a particular business. This can also help you make sure that you get what you think you're going to get in terms of your career and its progression, your training, your salary, and the company culture if you choose to accept their offer.

8 Things to Never Tell an Interviewer

An interview is an art of selling yourself in such a way that you can emphasize your strengths and can camouflage your weaknesses. No, it's not falsehood to hide what flaws you've. If you bring them to the notice of your interviewer, the only thing she would see is your "needed improvement" points. So, you need to focus more on your strengths and whatever weaknesses or lacks you feel you've; you need to manage tactically.

Candor is a beautiful word when we talk about an interview because it creates harmony between the interviewee and the interviewer. But while expressing everything candidly, certain things may pull a red flag for the interviewer. So, it's always better to be mindful of them and not tell them even while sharing your profile and your personal and professional life candidly with the interviewer.

We want you to perform at your highest in any interview. That's why we bring you things that matter while you're in the interview room but may have thought the way you should have. So, here are eight things you shouldn't tell an interviewer no matter how frankly you share yourself with him/her. And we will also discuss how you can camouflage it by saying certain things.

Things you should never tell an Interviewer;

I didn't include this job as I did it only for a short stint

Never say this in an interview room. If you ask us why, we would say that by saying this, you're proving to the interviewer that you're not trustworthy for the job s/he is offering, and thus no matter how skillful you become, you cannot step ahead and get this job. An interviewer is the first face of the company. And he will first think about his/her company, rather than taking an interest in you. Moreover, an interviewer is getting paid to protect his/her company and its interest, not you or your candidly expressed self-surrender. So, you also need to think about your benefits. You're there to get the job, not to impress or make friends with the interviewer. Be professional and share only that part that's necessary. Gulp the rest even it's coming out of your mouth.

In this case, if there's a gap and it's not mentioned, and you know that you did a job for a short duration during this time, wait for the interviewer to ask the question about the gap. You don't need to say anything without asking. If he asks to say that you took the time to prepare for the interviews at that time or say something like a physical ailment, but make sure that you've never mentioned the real truth in any of your profile – Facebook, Twitter, Linked-In, and elsewhere. If you've ever said that you've worked for a short duration, then you'll be caught.

It's always good not to lie. Thus whatever is necessary to mention, mention in your resume so that you don't need to lie.

I'd like to become _____ (something that's not aligned with the job you've applied for)

If you say this, you're doomed. Who wants you to recruit someone whose dreams are something else? If you're applying for a position of content writer and blabber that you want to become a professor, who will select you for the job? No-one will. So, be careful about this. All people are not your dream-flyers, and they're not interested in your dreams.

There're lots of interviewers who may say to you that we need to know who you want to be, and that's all we want to know so that we can place you in a suitable fit, but don't get trapped in that. They're saying this because they want to know the truth and not something edgy.

Know that there are two brains that we all have. One is neocortex, which is responsible for logic, and another is the limbic brain, the brain which controls your feelings. So, the recruiters who ask you this type of question is pointing toward your limbic brain. And without realizing it, you share your real feeling and guess what you're trapped.

When you're asked such a question, think about what you can be by holding this current job and prepare beforehand what you need to say. Maybe you need to say something like – "I believe when we sit on a car in the night, only thing we can see is another 2.5 inches; so right now that's what I want to see, and I want to learn as much as I can and want to stretch as much as I can. Hopefully, I will arrive at my dream destination because by choosing to dedicate myself to this job, I know in my heart that this is the right direction." If you say this, there would be nothing the recruiter can say, and the trick s/he has used wouldn't be working on you.

I'm sitting for an interview in various fields as of now

Are you mad? Saying the interviewer that you don't have clarity? See, the purpose of an interviewer is to select a candidate who will remain in the company for some time and not leave and go to another company for another job. Interviewers hate job-hoppers. All they want is to get a healthy return on investment by selecting you. If they don't see that there's a chance of getting a good ROI by selecting you, they won't.

So, never tell what you're doing in your professional life, especially when you're giving interviews in different fields. We understand that if you're fresher and you're confused about which career suits you best, you need to do some trial and error. Nothing is wrong in that. But don't show it to the interviewer. If s/he asks you about any other interview you're giving or not, tell him/her that you're focusing on this field, and you feel you're the right fit for this field as you believe you've all the qualities one should've to prosper in this area. And bang on! Interviewers have nothing more to say to you about that.

I want to move up quickly

Having ambition is not at all a bad thing. But if you understand what an interviewer wants from his/her ideal candidate, "I want to move up quickly" are not the phrases they want to hear. Because if you say so, they would feel that you want to grow faster so you'll not be stable, and if his/her company is not able to provide the growth you're looking for, you'll leave the job and search for another one. And that would drastically affect the output of the company (especially if it's an important position). So, never express your ambition in front of the interviewer. There may be another reason, but it's very subtle that you won't be able to decipher always. When you say such a thing, sometimes, the recruiter/interviewer who may be holding a prominent position feels threatened that you may quickly move up to his/her position. And guess what s/he acts out of that fear and would never give you a job and will call you "over-confident" or "over-ambitious."

You can, at best, say like – "I want to grow and stretch myself as much as I can, and I can see that this job would be able to provide me room for growth." If you say this, you're expressing yourself frankly, but hiding something that doesn't need to be said in front of the interviewer.

I don't have any references

Terrible statement to say to an interviewer!

An interviewer will never be satisfied with just you and your words. That's why there's a protocol for a background check if the position is a key position for the company. That's why they need people who can verify your background. If you say this to an interviewer, that means there's no way your statements can be tested, and thus if it's a key position, your chances of selection are very bleak.

So what to do if you don't have any references? Or suppose you're a fresher?

First of all, don't say it upfront. The interviewer may ask you about people who know you and your background. Think of at least three names before entering the interview room.

If you're fresher, think of 3 professors who would love to talk good about you. If you're somehow experienced, you should know someone whom you've worked with. Be careful while writing the names of the recommender in the application form. Make sure that they're trustworthy and would like you as much as to speak good about you. Remember, the interviewers will trust other people more than what you say about yourself.

My earlier job was a horrible one

Never say that to the interviewer. Why? Because it's a terrible statement! First of all, once you say this, you need to explain, and you need to do badmouthing about your previous employer. But the interviewer only can know about your words. The other side is hidden from him/her. So, how come s/he would believe that whatever you're saying is the truth? You may be a person who is very hard to work with, or maybe you've unrealistic expectations from a job or a boss.

So, if you feel that in your earlier job you did all your work properly and there's no room for you to do anything about it, then rephrase it in this way – "My previous job was a good one. I was excited. I did all I could. And my performance card also depicted the same. But right now, what I'm looking for is this (talk about the position you've applied for) as I believe there are certain limitations in my previous job profile."

The art is to say it, but as subtly as possible so that even the interviewer know what you're saying, there would be a doubt in his/her mind about whether what s/he understood is accurate or not. And you know you will always get the benefit of the doubt if you're outstanding in your work.

I'm applying at the university in the next summer

As typically as it may sound, interviewers want people who would like to stay in the company for at least more than a year! If not, then how the cost of recruitment would get sufficed and how the company would benefit from the recruitment drive?

There's no issue with education. But don't threaten the interviewer with the phrases like – "I'm going to join coming university year for this," and especially if it's a full-time course. If you feel that you'll be able to manage the job with your full-time study, it's always better not to say anything about it specifically during the interview. If you need to share this, say it after you get selected and say it with an assurance that you will maintain a clear distinction between your work and your study and your study would not hamper your work by any cost. So, don't talk about your education during your interview to play safe.

I'm waiting for someone to pick me up

Interviewers want people who are self-starters and who can create a ruckus with their actions. They don't like reactive people who even wait for someone to pick him/her up. Also, if it's real and you're from a conservative and protected family, ask your parents or husband to pick you up away from your interview place.

You don't want to show your potential boss that you need someone to pick you up, and you need someone to take your decision. It will create a wrong picture in their minds. Instead, once the interview is over, say 'thanks' to the receptionist and go away from the place. Go away from the location and connect the person who was about to pick you up from the interview place and ask them to come somewhere else.

The first impression is everything, and if you aren't able to create a first impression that will show you as proactive, responsible, and self-starter, probably you won't be able to get the job you want.

The above are the phrases which you should avoid saying by any cost. You understand that even many variations of these phrases are also capable of killing your dreams of getting a job you want. Pay heed to these and know where you might slip and prepare well. If you pay heed to the details, you will always do good in your interview.

Chapter 19: The Job Interview Process

Stay the course.

From starting gate to finish line, details matter.

Job Seeking Tasks

ALTHOUGH YOUR PARTICULAR CIRCUMSTANCES may vary, below are basic job-seeking tasks, from the particular motivating factor that started the process for you, all the way to accepting the position.

The job search process is complex, for which you'll need to multi-task and utilize among other talents, your:

research abilities;

communication and writing skills;

organizing aptitude; and

attention to detail.

An example of a motivating factor is that you want to earn money for school. So then...

You narrow down your employment choices, and think about options;

You consider your strengths, abilities, previous experiences, and interests;

Specific job options that suit your profile come into view;

You target employment possibilities in those areas for which you feel suited;

You research how to write a resume and cover letter, and you prepare them;

You create an application form template and record all necessary details;

You fill out job applications online and in person;

You follow up and remind employers that you're eager to be interviewed;

You respond to an invitation to attend an interview at a specific date and time, and confirm your attendance;

You record the details of the invitation phone call or email for future reference;

You practice answering typical interview questions;

You prepare your clothing for the interview;

You decide on the best travel option to get to the interview location;

You go to bed early the night before your interview;

You dress and groom yourself appropriately;

You ensure you've eaten and had sufficient water before your interview;

You arrive on time;

You introduce yourself to the greeter or receptionist;

You keep your focus while in the interview, and give it your best;

You email a thank you message to your interviewer;

You follow up several days to a week later;

You receive word on the outcome;

You accept the job offer!

Clothing Guidelines and Choices

Throughout your interview preparation, keep in mind that your grooming and clothing choices are leading factors in determining your success in landing the job.

When you attend an interview, you'll want to fit in, and appear as if you already work for the company. Make it easy for the interviewer to imagine you as their employee.

You can accomplish this if you conduct a bit of research beforehand to establish the company dress code and norms, including the colour palette, if they have one.

The dress code is easy to check out when you apply for a position in a retail store, restaurant, coffee shop, or other accessible worksite. If the company's employees wear a uniform, your best option is to dress in the colours of the company's uniform. The interviewer will notice that you're paying attention.

If it's difficult to pay a visit to the company due to location, security, or privacy concerns, don't be shy about making a telephone call to the company's main telephone number.

Mention to the person answering the call that you'll be attending a job interview and ask how employees at the company dress for that specific job. Then pull together interview clothing that follows that standard.

Keep Your Clothing Choices Simple.

Take care to gather your interview attire well in advance of your scheduled meeting. Check for missing buttons, torn hems, marks and stains, and proceed accordingly.

Even a little bit of discomfort with your shoes or clothing is guaranteed to deflate your confidence in an interview situation, where it's likely your level of self-consciousness will already be high.

Before purchasing any clothing items for an interview, check with friends and family members to see if they have what you need. Later, if you land the job, you can invest in clothing essentials for your work. For now, borrowed is good.

Interview Clothing Rules for Entry-Level Service and Trades Jobs that Should Never Be Broken

Never wear leggings to a job interview.

Never wear jogging pants, athletic pants, yoga pants, or shorts to a job interview unless you're applying for a job in a gym.

Never wear jeans with slashed knees, rips, or tears to a job interview.

Never wear low cut tops or revealing clothing to a job interview.

Never wear a tank top or sleeveless undershirt to a job interview.

Never wear a t-shirt with graphics to a job interview.

Never wear a hoodie to a job interview.

Never wear a baseball cap, knit cap, or toque to a job interview unless you're applying for a job on a ski hill or in a bicycle sales and repair shop.

Remove piercings. At the interview you can mention that you have piercings and ask about the company policy.

Long hair should be in a bun or knot, or tied back.

Minimal make-up.

Minimal jewelry. Men should not wear heavy wrist or neck chains.

Shoes should always be flat, with no open toes.

A jacket should always be worn or with you, unless it's a hot summer day.

Although street wear and casual attire — yoga pants, tank tops, leggings, jogging pants, and hoodies — are now commonplace, street wear and casual attire aren't acceptable clothing choices to wear when dropping off application forms, or for attending a job interview, no matter how casual or informal the setting might be.

And no matter what anyone else has told you.

Interview Clothing Suggestions for Specific Jobs

Animal care — jeans or cotton slacks, t-shirt or collared long-sleeved shirt or blouse, casual shoes

Automotive — jeans, t-shirt or collared long-sleeved shirt or blouse, dark runners or work boots

Bakery — white long-sleeved shirt or black or white t-shirt, dark pants, casual shoes or runners

Bike shop, ski shop – jeans or cotton slacks, t-shirt, runners or casual shoes

Coffee shop – white or black long-sleeved shirt or t-shirt, black pants, casual shoes

Construction – jeans, dark t-shirt, runners, work boots, or casual shoes

Dollar store – white or neutral long-sleeved shirt or blouse, dark pants, casual shoes

Fast food – white long-sleeved shirt or blouse or white t-shirt, dark pants, casual shoes

Grocery store – long-sleeved shirt or blouse, jacket, dark pants, casual shoes

Gym or community centre – athletic pants, dark t-shirt, runners

Hospitality, hotel – white or black collared shirt or blouse, jacket, black dress pants, black shoes.

Spa – white long-sleeved shirt or blouse, black pants, black shoes

Landscaper – jeans, t-shirt, dark runners, work boots, or casual shoes

Lumber and hardware retailer – jeans or casual pants, collared shirt, dark runners or work boots

Movie theatre – white or neutral long-sleeved shirt or blouse, dark pants, casual shoes

Office and professional – dark suit and tie/jacket, white or pastel shirt or blouse, dress shoes

Pizza restaurant – white or black t-shirt, dark jeans or pants, casual shoes

Restaurant – white collared shirt or blouse, black pants, black shoes

Retail – white or neutral long-sleeved shirt or blouse, dark dress pants or skirt, black shoes

Service – white long-sleeved shirt or blouse, dark dress pants, black shoes

Swamping, delivery – jeans, dark t-shirt, runners or work boots.

After you're hired, you can follow whatever company norms apply, but...

at the application form and interview stages it's important not to make assumptions about what's acceptable.

It's better to err on the side of caution.

The Information Interview

If you want first-hand information about a particular job in which you have an interest pursuing, an information interview is an excellent way to gather the inside details.

As a first step, do a bit of research to determine the best person with whom to meet. When you have decided who that person is, call the company and obtain his or her email address.

Compose a brief email requesting a fifteen-minute meeting to conduct an interview with them to gather information. You should stress that you're not seeking employment, but are looking for information to assist you in determining your future career direction. If the y respond favourably to your request, set a time, and prepare your questions.

Information interviews in the service, hospitality, retail, construction, trades, and automotive sectors tend to be casual in nature, and rarely exceed fifteen minutes in length.

There's a chance you'll be standing during the interview, in an area where business is conducted, often with customers present.

In office, sales, and professional settings, information interviews are typically conducted in a private office or in an area away from clients and employees. Information interviews in these settings tend to range from fifteen to thirty minutes in length.

Make a point to arrive ten minutes early for your information interview, suitably dressed, with a number of questions you've prepared. If you're uncertain about appropriate attire for the interview, refer to the information listed above under the heading Interview Clothing Suggestions for Specific Jobs.

Questions for the information interview should focus on a specific job for which you have an interest, the skill level, training, and experience required to do the job, typical employment opportunities in the field, pro's and con's, and any advice the person you're interviewing can give you about entering that particular field.

During the information interview, it's your responsibility to lead the discussion, and you should be ready to ask questions that you've prepared and brought with you.

Keep your eye on the time. Unless you're gathering information for an office or professional job, wrap up within the fifteen-minute time period.

In any case, if the person you're interviewing appears to be rushed or distracted, ask your most pertinent questions, keep the energy moving, and conclude the interview early on a high note.

Initiate closure by extending your hand for a handshake, thank them for their time, and leave.

As soon as you're able, compose and send a brief email with Thank you in the subject line, similar to this example:

Dear _____,

Thank you for spending time with me today and answering my questions about _____. You have given me a lot to think about, and I am grateful for all of your suggestions and information!

Regards, _____

Information interviews are an excellent way for you to gather insight into a job within a particular field, to get a sense of current and future opportunities, and to explore the major employers in that field. Asking for information will give you first-hand experience, and the entire process can be a confidence builder.

Visiting varied workplaces offers a window into the ways in which organizations do business, and provides you with a sense of the other side of the desk, that you can call on when you prepare for future job interviews.

There's no limit to the number of information interviews you can conduct in any field, and although it's best not to return to speak to someone else in the same company for at least three months, the sky is the limit if you decide to query varied organizations in the same or other areas of interest.

Leading Up to The Job Interview

At least two days before your job interview, launder, iron, and prepare your clothing and shoes.

Assemble your documents - application template, 2 copies of your resume, and 2 reliable pens.

Determine your transit route, or confirm the parking availability if you'll be driving.

The night before the interview, ensure that you get to bed early and have plenty of sleep.

The day of the interview, pay attention to grooming – nails, hair, beard.

Make sure to eat and drink water prior to the interview.

Keep yourself calm – use positive imaging and self-talk.

What to Take to the Interview

A zippered case or satchel to hold your documents and pens;

Two pens (one is a back-up, just in case);

Two copies of your resume in a large envelope (one copy for you, one for your interviewer);

Two copies of your reference page;

Pre-filled application form to use as a template;

Copies of your certificates or letters of accomplishment, in a separate large envelope;

Remember to also take with you:

Your notebook;

Neatly written questions about the specific job and the company that you can refer to at the end of the interview, when your interviewer asks if you have any questions;

Directions, transit information to the interview;

Company telephone number (so you can call to postpone in case an emergency occurs while you're on your way).

Conclusion

Thank you for making it through to the end of this book. Who knows what nerve-wracking interview could become the job of your dreams! Now that you are aware of all the things that you might be asked, it's time to practice!

Have others ask you these questions so you can give answers out loud. Rewrite some of the questions we asked in ways that the interviewer might ask if they were to change things up. Think of new answers, and remember the meaning and not just the order of the words that you want to say.

You've familiarized yourself with the frequent must-know interview questions and the frequent unexpected interview questions. You should now feel confident answering those boring interview questions with a passion and excitement that your interview will appreciate, and you should also feel comfortable tackling those dreadful or unexpected question without hesitation.

Now it's time to prove it. Review the chapters of this book from time to time to stay brushed up on some excellent interview questions. But most importantly, apply what you've learned from this book to your next interview. You've learned how to flawlessly exceed your interviewer's expectations and how to market yourself as the ideal candidate, so go forth and do so.

www.ingramcontent.com/pod-product-compliance
Lightning Source LLC
Chambersburg PA
CBHW072007070526
44583CB00015B/1379